Sea-Change

Wivenhoe remembered

Sea-Change

Wivenhoe remembered

Paul Thompson

with

Teresa Crompton, Brenda Corti,
Don Smith and Janet Turner

TEMPUS

Frontispiece: *Fixing the stern frame at James Cook's, c.1970: Jack Taylor. (John Bines)*

First published 2006

Tempus Publishing Limited
The Mill, Brimscombe Port,
Stroud, Gloucestershire, GL5 2QG

British Library Cataloguing in Publication Data.
A catalogue record for this book is available from the British Library.

ISBN 0 7524 3967 7

Typesetting and origination by Tempus Publishing Limited
Printed in Great Britain

Contents

Acknowledgements   6

Introduction   8

one   Ernie Vince: a Life on the Quay and the Water   11

two   Farming and Social Hierarchy   19

three   The Riverside   31

four   Factories, Shops, and Pubs   49

five   Professions, Services and the Churches   67

six   Societies and Clubs   79

seven   Childhood and Family Lives   95

eight   New People   111

nine   Narratives of Change: War, Local Politics and Struggles   127

ten   Still Sailing the Colne   143

eleven James Dodds: a New Fusion   153

        Book Contributors   157

Acknowledgements

This book is the outcome of 'Remembering Wivenhoe,' a community oral history project which has been based on voluntary contributions of many kinds. Most crucial of all have been over 190 people listed at the end of this book, whose memories have been recorded for the project and for the benefit of all interested in the history of Wivenhoe in the future. We are deeply grateful to them, and to all those others who have given their time, knowledge and energy to make the fulfilment of the project possible.

The project has been directed by Paul Thompson and administered by Brenda Corti, and the project committee have also included Annie Bielecka, Ken Plummer, Don Smith, Janet Turner, and (chair) the Rev David Thomas. Jacqueline Thomas as library representative was succeeded by Jane Stanley.

At the core of the project was an enthusiastic and talented interviewing team, some experienced, some new to recording life stories: Lisa Baxter, Libby Bishop, Annie Bielecka, Ann Clarke, Brenda Corti, Ellie Crichton Stuart, Ann Dale, Shirley Dow, Bruce Gant, Diana Gittins, Marcel Glover, Alison Kent, Caroline Munn-Giddings, Carol Mitchell, Helen Polom, Kate Powis, Lin Roberts, Brian Sinclair, Tony Swift, Paul Thompson and Jan Thurlow.

In the early months of the project there was also a parallel research group, which provided valuable historical background information, consisting of Elizabeth Baines, Ann Clarke, Pat Marsden and Janet Turner. We also were also very much helped with maritime historical information by Bill Ellis.

Our earlier presentations of material from the project were particularly helped by the technical and audio skills of Marcel Glover and Janet Turner, and by Don Smith's collecting of photographs. For illustrations we were also generously helped by Colin Andrews, John Bines, Joyce Blackwood, the Congregational Church, Tim Denham, James Dodds, Peter and Diane Duffield, Phil Faucheux, Tony Forsgate, Jan Frostick, Marcel Glover, Marjorie Goldstraw, Annabel Gooch, Betty Govan, Ken Green, Pat Green, Peter Green, Jean Harding, Frank Hodgson, Glendower Jackson, Kitty Funnel, Dennis Marsden, Ralph Moss, Sue Murray, the Nottage Institute, Ellen Primm, John Stewart, Don Smith, Janet Turner, Ernie Vince, Graham Wadley, and Dave and Sylvia Weatherall.

In launching the project we were especially helped by support from Andrew Philips and Colchester Recalled, the Wivenhoe Town Council, the Sociology Department at the University of Essex, the Friends of St Mary's, the Sailing Club, Millfields School and Broomgrove School.

Finally, for their crucial financial support we thank the Heritage Lottery Fund for their grant of £43,000 which has made the project possible. We also received a grant of £2,750 from Professsor Ivor Crewe, Vice-Chancellor of the University of Essex, which enabled us to include some interviews with early university staff members. The Heritage Lottery Fund grant has in particular enabled the skilled transcription of the interviews by Marion Haberhauer, the production of a DVD by Steve Humphries, Andy Attenburrow and Mike Pharey of Testimony Films (which we are launching with the book), and the appointment of Teresa Crompton to assist in writing the book and in the archiving of the interviews.

The interviews will archived as be part of the 'Colchester Recalled' collection and can be consulted at either Colchester Museum or the University of Essex Library, and also at the Essex Sound Archive. We are also intending for a more extended series of thematic extracts from the interviews, edited by Teresa Crompton, to be made available through the Wivenhoe website.

Some other books on recent Wivenhoe history

The most comprehensive account of Wivenhoe in the twentieth century, particularly strong on industry and social organisations, is Nicholas Butler, *The Story of Wivenhoe* (1989). Dick Barton, *Wivenhoe: Its Attractions, Pleasures and Eccentric Natives* (1975) gives another briefer and spicier general picture. Janet Cooper with Shirley Durgan and C.C. Thornton, *Victoria County of Essex,* Vol X, has a very interesting entry on Wivenhoe. The maritime aspect of Wivenhoe's life is recounted in John Leather, *The North Seamen* (1971) and *The Salty Shore* (1979), and Margaret Leather, *Saltwater Village* (1977) gives the parallel Rowhedge story. David Craze, *Wivenhoe: a Portrait in Pictures* (1998) records many of the visual changes up to the mid-century. On more detailed themes, the many interesting local publications include Rosemary Feesey, *Wivenhoe Park. A History of the House and Grounds* (1963); Paul Brown, *The Wivenhoe and Brightlingsea Railway* (1965); on the gravel pit, Bill Loveless, *Destiny Delayed* (2003); C.G. Ellis, *Nottage. A Viking Influence on Wivenhoe Quay* (1984); Peter Kay, *Wivenhoe Pubs* (2003); Rev Clementina Gordon, *Wivenhoe Congregational Church* (1966); Geoffrey King, *'We nearly closed': A History of Wivenhoe Methodist Church* (1980s); and Leonard Drinkell, *Colne Lodge No 2477: The First Hundred Years* (1993).

A note on boundaries

Many people with homes in Wivenhoe have spent their lives working in Colchester or London, and some much further away, as sailors or soldiers, as colonial administrators in India or teachers in Africa. Here, however, we focus on their Wivenhoe-based working and lives. But rather than confining ourselves to the administrative boundaries, which during our period have shrunk on the north side and expanded on the east, the history described here is of a 'greater Wivenhoe,' which includes the whole of the Wivenhoe Park Estate, the gravel pit and farms on the east side, and the Colne estuary to Brightlingsea and beyond.

Introduction

This book tells the story of how Wivenhoe has changed since the inter-war years, through to the 1980s, and with reflections from present-day perspectives. In the last eighty years a small riverside industrial village of little more than 2,000 people has grown to a town of 10,000, lost most of its industry and many of its shops, but gained a community of artists and the university. This is an oral history of Wivenhoe in this time of profound change, told here through the voices of its own people, the men and women, both locally-born and newcomers, older and younger, who have experienced these transforming times.

Oral history is spoken history, and the rhythms and patterns of speech are not the same as those of written English. In editing from the memories recorded for this project, we have condensed and tightened most extracts, but we have kept the grammar and turns of phrase and lyricism of oral speech, thus keeping our texts closer and truer to the spoken record.

One of the major strengths of oral history is that it can bring in evidence from a much wider social range than is possible from written sources, bringing a variety of perspectives on the same social changes. Thus landowning families are richly documented in the record offices, but here we have been able to bring in witness from among their domestic servants and their ploughmen. Similarly, we can match the skilled shipyard craftsman with his apprentice, the shopkeeper with the delivery boy, the clergyman with the choirboy, the yachtsman with the yachtswoman. Oral history is equally valuable in giving us an almost unique access to many hidden aspects of the history of everyday life: for example, changing work culture, or leisure activities, or the world of childhood play.

Oral history also raises the question of memory. Certainly everyone's memory is at least to some extent reshaped over time by personal experience. Fortunately research has shown that memory is strongest and most reliable for experiences which are regularly repeated, and this includes many of the themes we cover here, such as the experiences of work or family relationships. Conversely, memories of once-only events, such as accounts of local conflicts, need to be read much more cautiously.

Sometimes, however, factual accuracy is not the main interest of a testimony. Very often stories and anecdotes are carrying a social message; such as the railway engine drivers whose off-duty tales of semi-mythical exploits tell us so eloquently of the drivers' pride in their work skills. Other memories represent feelings and opinions, and it does not matter at all if these are different from those of other people; on the contrary, our sense of the varying experience of social change comes precisely from these contrasts.

In the chapters which follow, we look at changes in different aspects of Wivenhoe life: the farms, the riverside, factories, shops and so on. But let us begin with some overall views of the changing village, bringing out how there is no single story of Wivenhoe since the 1920s, but rather a series of perspectives, varying by age, position and experience. The first (exceptionally in this book) is from a written autobiography, *Destiny Delayed*, by Bill Loveless, born in 1921, whose father ran the gravel pit, and the last three from ten-year-olds are from a workshop held by the project at Broomgrove School in May 2006.

Some Views of Changing Wivenhoe from the 1920s to the 1980s

In the late 1920s it could be called a rather non-descript sort of village: with a stratum of discontent because of decline in the River Colne shipbuilding prosperity of the war years; and a more narrow, rather clique-like discontent that the days of fitting out and serving on rich men's yachts were also drawing to an end. A few of the middle class proper there were in the village: two doctors, the Rector, an occasional person of culture and means, and one or two business men. Most of its inhabitants would now be called lower middle class, working in hum-drum jobbing, retailing or clerical capacities. Art-loving, riverside, semi-Bohemian Wivenhoe had yet to come.

Bill Loveless

I always felt Wivenhoe had four different types of people. First of all there were the people who worked in the Shipyard. When I went to Wivenhoe first of all, the Shipyard was very active. Another part of Wivenhoe was the University which I think, when I first went there, was still going through slightly trying times. And the third group were the commuters, the people who worked out of Wivenhoe in Colchester or London, they were tied, totally, to the railway. And then the fourth group, what I would just call the old Wivenhoe people that had always lived there. I always felt that in many ways Wivenhoe was wonderfully classless.

Canon Stephen Hardie

Greasy cafes to delicatessens

Some of the original Wivenhoe families did regret the fact that the town had expanded so enormously. There was a lot of looking back, by them, to the greasy cafes – the Lucy Dee, next to the Black Buoy, used to be a greasy cafe where you'd be able to find loads of men from the shipyard, having their bacon and eggs in the morning, in a steamy atmosphere, just like in a city. And all of that started fading away, and becoming delicatessens and antique shops, to accommodate more the incomer. The incomers, however, like me, were so thrilled to be in this place, we wanted to make it our home, and wanted to be part of it, and I think over the twenty-seven years I've been here, what has evolved, is that the people who have come in, have loved Wivenhoe so much that they will sing its praises across the world.

Janita Lefevre

Lost friendliness

I used to love Wivenhoe with a passion, and that's totally gone now. It's getting bigger and bigger and bigger, and the villageness about it has gone. There's no shops, there's no heart to the place any more. People were more friendly. When I first moved to where I live now, people just didn't speak to me up there. It's still a nice place to live but it's just not what it used to be. You can walk in a crowded pub and feel very lonely, which is a weird feeling when I always think it's like 'my village.'

Rodney Bowes

Enjoying new people

I like to see new people around. I've got some new neighbours moved in from London, which I'm very happy with. Let's face it, it's not right, is it, that in my age group, I should be too critical of all these young people coming in. I'm pleased a lot of the new people are getting involved in things, like in the Council, with the Wivenhoe Society, the Sailing Club. They've got to find their own levels and settle in, haven't they?

Don Smith

Three Ten-Year-Olds' Views Today

It has lots of places to play in but it's very busy and has lots of traffic. The woods are excellent and the field next to where I live is a great place to walk my dog. But some things are not so good like the future skatepark on the field. I don't really like all the houses being built at the Quay. I would love to have lived in the past because children had so much more freedom and no one had to go into town because there were so many more shops. Although I can't imagine life without a car, TVs, radios and computers.

Charlotte Gruender

I like Wivenhoe because it has good parks and woods and it has nice people that help you and you can play anywhere in the woods. A game that we play is manhunt and you can play Knock Down Ginger.

Aaron Wood

Wivenhoe seems to me as if it's remote countryside, a village. I love the way the river sparkles as if stardust has been scattered on it by friendly angels. In the summer it's really nice to go down to the park, and then get some fish and chips by the Quay. It's amazing to think that great steam trains rode past the woods every day! I think it would have been really cool to live when many of our grand-parents lived here. It seems so weird that children were allowed to go *anywhere* they wanted!!! I can't believe that they got up to much mischief. I'd have loved to see what school was like and meet the dreaded Miss Smith in person!

Holly Joscelyne

one

Ernie Vince:
a Life on the Quay
and the Water

Ernie Vince. (Paul Thompson)

I was born in 1911 at a little farm between Elmstead and Crockleford. Then I came to Wivenhoe when I was six years old, and lived on the Quay. My father was in the First World War. We lived next door to my father's parents, grandfather was a farm worker. My mother's father was gamekeeper for Bentley Hall. Yes, I used to go there for my school holidays! I used to enjoy going there. And then, unfortunately, the family broke up, and my mother took the children down to Wivenhoe, and left my father at Crockleford.

I didn't see him after that. No. No. Well, I must add, he treated me terribly. I used to have beatings galore, had a terrible time. At first, the authorities wouldn't let mother have me, they made me stay with him. But I ran away. Then the authorities came and grabbed me and took me back to Crockleford, but I wouldn't stay. I ran again. They had to let mother have me. That was the end of the family story, in that sense. Eventually my father passed away, of course. I was in the Mediterranean in a big yacht when I got a telegram from my mother to say he was passed on, and that was that.

When I came to Wivenhoe, first we lived in one of the cottages on the Quay they call 'The Folly.' Then my mother was able to get a house on her own, and we moved into Alma Street. I had three sisters and one brother, and the house was only two bedrooms. My mother worked for a private family, as a house cleaner. And then when the fish factories opened up, she got a job there, sorting the fish. Oh, she was very nice. Very small person. Much different to me!

From school to sea

Almost immediately, from the time I went to live on the Quay, I made my mind up I was going on the water. Well, my old Uncle Charlie Sainty on my mother's side kept the ferry then, and I used to get the ferry boat, and if he wasn't about, I'd go off across the ferry and get a passenger. He taught me how to row properly, he taught me how to scull, all sorts of boat work. So I got to know how to use a boat quite early.

Before I left school, when I was about eleven years old, the Nottage Institute was then held in a room over the house next door to the Black Buoy pub, and Captain Abraham Harvey, he lived up Anglesea Road, he was the Navigation and Seamanship Master, and I started going there. He taught me an awful lot, he taught me all I knew about navigation and seamanship.

I'd made up my mind I was going to sea, and our local doctor then, Dr Kevin, owned a cruiser/racer yacht. I went to see the doctor to ask for a job as a boy seaman aboard. And so it was accepted, my mother said 'Yes,' and I left school on the Friday, and went to sea on the Saturday! Then we raced at Ramsgate on the Sunday! I'll always remember that! And then we carried on round the coast for the summer, doing the various races. That was my start in the yachting business.

As a boy seaman, I had to scrub the decks in the morning, and clean the brass, then get the sails, get ready for racing, if it was a race day. Captain Cranfield of Rowhedge was the skipper. There were a crew of three. The doctor always sailed the ship, when he was aboard, for racing. When the doctor was sailing the ship, the captain kept a general eye on things, advised him about tactics, which was usually what racing skippers did do if the owner sailed. And all I did was keep quiet! Did what I was told! Mrs Kevin did the cooking. She was a Rowhedge lady.

We sailed all around the British coast, as far up as on to the Clyde, the usual cruiser racing season, amongst all the big classes. We started off at Ramsgate, then continued on down to do Cowes Week, and from my memory, we didn't race after Cowes. Then down to the West Country, Dartmouth, Plymouth, and Torbay. Then up round, up and on to the Clyde. After the Clyde we came down the east side, when we came home at the end of the season. We came home, and laid the yacht up.

Fishing for sprats

So I had the season there, and then in the winter-time, I went fishing and sprat catching in one of

Charlie Sainty senior, ferryman, with cyclist, c. 1935. (Glendower Jackson)

the local boats. With two brothers named Gunn – that's one of the old Wivenhoe fishing families. My first winter's fishing was with them. They had an ordinary smack, with the auxiliary motor, they'd all got engines in by then. Crew of three. I was working the nets, shooting the nets, getting the nets, unloading the fish. They called it 'stowboating.' Brightlingsea was the main port, then, because most of it was barrelled and pickled and exported to Russia and Germany.

On Rosabelle

The next summer I went into – you've heard of the *Rosabelle*, no doubt, haven't you? I went in the *Rosabelle,* and I was in her for two years then. The captain was Captain Harvey, Wivenhoe man. She was a big steamer, 600-ton steamer, but she always laid up at Wivenhoe at the end of the summer season, and at about the end of March/early April, we put all the equipment back aboard, and we'd be fit out for the Mediterranean cruise. Then come back about the end of June, so they were back to

go to Cowes. And then we cruised again, and then came back home, laid up. And, of course, it was back to fishing again in the winter. So I had two seasons in her.

There were a crew of twenty-eight on *Rosabelle*. I was AB – Able Seaman – in the first year I was there. Deck scrubbing, cleaning brass, and keeping watch when you were at sea, keeping watch for your spell at steering and look-out keeping. Four hours on and four off. I remember one time I was frightened. We got caught out in *Rosabelle* for seventy-two hours, hove to about sixty miles off the Portuguese coast one time. And again another time later on, in *Sunbeam*, oh, she was a terror, she would roll! *Sunbeam* had three big steel masts, they weighed thirteen ton each, and when you got beam to it, oh, she was rail to rail! We got caught about forty or fifty miles off Gibraltar, we were bound into the Med and we got caught this night – and it was bad, I must admit – she was all awash. We lost one boat overboard, washed out the davits, on the quarterdeck. But anyhow, we got over that. They were about the two worst moments, I think.

Left:
Theodore Pim, stockbroker, owner of Rosabelle II. *(Nottage)*

Below:
Rosabelle II *laid up in Wivenhoe for the winter, with* Vanessa, Gunreda *and* Venetia. *(Nottage)*

Rosabelle was split up into sections. There was a fo'c'sle [forecastle], where the deckhands, the ABs and so on, and the fireman, slept, lived in the fo'c'sle. They had their own fo'c'sle cook. Then the officers in the mess room next door, they had their own steward and their meals were all cooked in the main galley. The owner and his guests were in the dining saloon. There were always probably half a dozen aboard, different friends of the owner. They had a music room, and Mrs Pim used to play the piano sometimes.

We used to go straight from Brightlingsea to Cannes, and then get the ship cleaned up, ready for them to join, and from Cannes, down through to the Greek Islands, and then we'd cross over to Alexandria, come back by Algiers, Morocco, and all along the North African coast. Then it was time to come home. Then we'd get ready again, and they'd be off up to the Baltic for the later summer. There, from home, we'd go straight up to Copenhagen. Then from Copenhagen, we'd go across to Stavanger and Bergen, right up to the North Cape, through the fjords, you go inside the islands all the way up, but it was compulsory to have a pilot in those days. It was lovely, beautiful

ROSABELLE   GUNDREDA   VANESSA   VENETIA

scenery, and we were getting all the pleasures and being paid for it!

Then, unfortunately, Mr Pim the owner passed away. He was one of the founders of the English Stock Exchange. He was a lovely old gentleman. Mr Pim would always talk to you on the deck. Not all owners would talk to the crew. No, you were just somebody who they had to pay to work for them! But that all came to an end. When Mr Pim died, we were all left in his will, everybody.

Lord Runciman's *Sunbeam II*

So after *Rosabelle*, I went back to fishing again that winter. Then we'd laid up, we'd finished fishing, and I was down on the quayside, and another fisherman friend from Tollesbury was walking along the Quay, and he told me a captain from Tollesbury was looking for a ship's crew to join a brand new big three-masted schooner being built in Scotland, *Sunbeam II* – belonging to the Lord Runciman. So we took her down to Southampton, then got ready for the summer cruise. She wasn't a racing schooner, *Sunbeam*, oh no, she was a 700-tons cruising schooner. She had a big crew. We had thirty-eight aboard her, three of us from Wivenhoe, because there was sailing most of the time, although she had an auxiliary.

We did much the same cruising, in *Sunbeam*, as we did in *Rosabelle* in previous years. And then came back to Cowes for Cowes Week – like most people did with the big ships in those days, it was *the* thing to be at Cowes! In those days, there was loads going on at Cowes, hundreds and hundreds of yachts of all sizes and shapes, plus all the racing. They went to Cowes for the social part of it. There was quite a crowd of guests aboard, sometimes a dozen, besides Lord Runciman and his wife. Lord Runciman was an old square rig ship man himself, and if you were at the wheel and he'd come along, he'd say, 'Let her luff up a bit,' thinking he's giving you some instructions! But you didn't take any notice of that, because the captain was the only man you took orders from.

The first time I had my own smack, *Christine*

After *Sunbeam*, we was back to fishing again, of course, for the winter. That's all there was to do. North Sea Canners, they'd started up by then – Mr Worsp – and they'd had a new smack built at Brightlingsea, *Christine* was her name, and he asked me if I'd take the *Christine*. So we went to the launch of her, and I worked there for all the winter. That's the first time I had my own smack. And worked there for the winter, spratting again. And then it was back to *Sunbeam* again in the summer.

Silver Foam, *Caretta* and Gifford of the YMCA

Then after that I became skipper for a man, named Gifford, the international secretary of the YMCA. We looked at one or two yachts, and he bought *Silver Foam*, a little fifteen-ton yawl, a lovely little thing. But because of his job, travelling all over the world to conferences, the sailing yacht, really, was not quite the thing, and so after the second year, he decided that he'd go in for power. He bought a sixty-ton motor yacht, all teak, built in Scotland, called the *Caretta*. So we started motor boating. I'm a sailor man, really, at heart, but it was a job.

That went on till the winter of 1938-39, when he was taken very ill – the owner. He said, 'I'll keep you on. But, you'll have to pay the crew off and explain to them.' Which wasn't very pleasant! Having to tell the chaps they haven't got a job. And I hadn't got a job, actually, only messing about aboard the boat, there was nothing to do.

Alan Colman and *Wishbone*: 1939

Then he contacted me one day. He was very friendly with the Colman family – the mustard people. And he said, 'I've had Mr Alan Colman on to me. His Scotch skipper has left him, and he's got no one for the season. Would you be interested?' So I said, 'Oh yes.' So I took the schooner – *Wishbone*

— Mr Colman's yacht, and fitted out at his own berth and boat-building shops on the Broads. She was a beautiful thing to sail, a gaff rig schooner. She was actually the first all-welded British steel yacht. The very first one that was all welded steel. She was very fast.

So I joined her. There were four of us. Anyhow, we fitted out and set off for the Baltic. Of course, we did some miles! His object was to get to Petrograd — or St Petersburg they call it now. But that didn't work out! He didn't sail from Lowestoft with us, out to the Baltic. I took the yacht up to Stockholm, and he flew out to Stockholm and joined us, and then we cruised about the Gulf of Finland. We got as far as Kotka, which is a very big timber port on the Finnish/Russian border. And on this particular day at Kotka, he said, 'Tomorrow, if everything's all right, we'll sail up the last few miles up to Petrograd.'

So off they went ashore on their day's sightseeing and, and he said, 'We'll be back about five.' But at midday, one of the chaps was on deck and called out, 'The Guv'nor is on the quay, waving like the devil.' So I said, 'All right. Well, get the launch and go and get him.' So they packed him off aboard. He said, 'Ernie, war is imminent.' He said, 'We're advised to get back to England as quickly as we can.' So he said, 'I've booked a flight from Helsinki. You get underway as quickly as you can, and get back.'

So after they'd gone, we packed our lashings down, and got ready to go to sea, and we left Kotka for home. On the way, we called at Copenhagen, and I put a bit more fuel in the auxiliary tank, in case we had to do a lot of motoring across the North Sea. In the meantime, while we laid alongside the quay, the Copenhagen harbourmaster came along, and I said to him, 'All right if we lay here for the night?' He said, 'Skipper, I wouldn't stay another minute if I were you.' He said, 'It's definitely going to happen any minute.' I said, 'Well, if that's your advice, we'll push off.' Which we did.

As we were going out to the Skaggerack, there was loads of big German trawlers going out, all off

mine-laying. And when we got out in the North Sea, we had a lot of fog and no wind! We had to motor a lot of the time.

We got back to Lowestoft at midnight on the Thursday, and war was declared on the Sunday morning. So we escaped that all right — just.

Wartime

Then, of course, we put all the gear in the store over the weekend, and went home. We didn't know what we were going to do! But very soon somebody roped me in as an ambulance driver. Then the Admiralty decided to commandeer *Caretta* and offered me the command of her as a coastal patrol vessel. So I agreed. I spent about eighteen months on coastal patrol. We'd go to sea for so many days, and then I don't know what we were supposed to do if anything happened! They painted her with the old cowpat colour and put a couple of guns aboard her, and there again, was all strange crew, strangers from here, there and everywhere.

Then at *HMS Nemo*, at Brightlingsea, they set up an air/sea rescue service, under Commander Campbell. They gave me a high speed American motor yacht. They put five crew aboard, and they'd send us off to sea, three days at a time on patrol, just waiting for people to fall in the sea! Doing a lifeboatman's job really. That went on until we were so advanced in Europe, it wasn't necessary any more. I picked up 163 chaps who were alive and all right — not too badly injured. But we picked up a lot of poor devils we were too late for. Unfortunately, putting it bluntly, more dead ones than alive ones.

Last yachting years

Then when I was discharged, I went back to my original yacht owner Mr Colman. They found *Caretta* but she was in a such a state he didn't want her back. Instead he bought a big sailing ketch called *Polaris*, she was German-built, sixty-five-ton. So we carried on the usual cruising in the summertime, south coast across to the other side – Amsterdam, Ostend and those sort of places, we didn't go so far then – and pottering about in the boatyard in the wintertime. Then in about 1956 my owner died, and so that ended my yachting career. It left me trying to think out what to do. But then Green came along with his offer, they wanted to buy a trawler, and would I be interested in taking it?

Fishing and winter yard work

The boatyard never did any good much, there was not enough yachting in Wivenhoe, really, to make it a viable concern. Mr Colman had bought the 'Penny Stores' [in the late 1930s] so people could store their boats away in the winter time. There wasn't enough work about Wivenhoe, repair work, to make it really viable. But we did get a lot of boats to store, we were always full of boats in the wintertime. So that's what my winter occupation became. I didn't go fishing any more, it stopped for quite a while. Then in 1955, they decided to give it up, put it on the market.

Then Mr Harding, from West Mersea, he bought it, but only on condition that I would stay there as well. But he wanted to start building, that was his aim. So he did, and they built some lovely yachts there too, over the years. Then, unfortunately, he died very suddenly. When Mr Harding died, then I went back to fishing.

The Green Brothers had bought a trawler in Ireland, a fifty-footer, with a brand new Rolls-Royce engine. I went back over to Ireland and got her, and I stayed with them until I retired, at sixty-five. We were general trawling in the summertime, like for sole and whiting, and anything of that sort, plaice. In the wintertime, we were herring fishing, with a special net called a 'Larsen Trawl.' I was with them seven years.

After I retired, I still used to potter about down at the boatyard, and mess about on the Quay. So I

Ernie Vince launching a boat designed by Dr Radcliffe, from Stanley Cook's Yard, 1937. (John Stewart)

always found something to do. In the house I can do anything. I can cook, launder, what you like.

I married in 1937, to Alice Hatch. She was a local girl, they were ten in family. She worked in Cook's Shipyard for twenty years, cooking in the canteen. And the day I retired, she retired as well! She said, 'If you're leaving off, so am I!' We just had two daughters. For over fifty years we lived in Hamilton Road. Much later, when I was a widower, I shared house with Mrs Warner, widow of Captain Warner.

On the barges: sail was always my love

For a four or five years in the early 1930s I'd worked on the big coastal sailing barges, beginning as mate for Captain Ted Warner. It was the usual coastal work, London, Ipswich, Felixstowe, Colchester. Mrs Warner spent a lot of time aboard the barge as well. She loved it, yes! She left the house on its own and came aboard the barge! She loved sailing in the barge.

What sort of cargoes? Mostly any timber, cottonseed, but it was chiefly cereals, chiefly wheat. We sailed day and night. We had to work to the tides. The tides were your greatest aids as well as the wind, unless the wind was in the correct direction, you couldn't do much against the tide, you didn't make much progress then. I liked the barging, because it was sailing again. It was marvellous how they would go, if the conditions were right, oh, they would go all right. But going to wind was a bit of a slow job, very often. It's amazing how well they did sail, really. Sail was always my love, really and truly!

two

Farming and
Social Hierarchy

Charles Gooch leading the hunt. (Annabel Gooch)

The Farms and the Village

In the 1950s Wivenhoe remained, as it had been for centuries, as much a farming as a maritime village, with six farms occupying most of its hinterland, and still part of everyday village life.

Cattle in the village: the slaughterhouse and greengrocery

The slaughterhouse was down the bottom of Blyths Lane, which is opposite the church. It's still got the rings in the wall where they used to tie the bullocks up before they killed them. And on Saturdays, about lunchtime, cattle trucks would come to Wivenhoe, and the drover would, with his stick, go in and drive off maybe four or five cows or bullocks. And cattle aren't daft – they knew they were going down to the slaughter-house. Maybe they could smell the blood from the slaughterhouse. And you'd always get one says, 'I'm not going down there!' and he would turn and run through the churchyard. That was great fun! All the boys down on the Quay, all over the place, chasing the bullock along the Quay, up through Anchor Hill, and round by the station, to bring the bullocks back to the slaughterhouse! And the drovers would give you maybe sixpence for bringing one back. It was great fun! Yes, great fun!

Glendower Jackson

When I first left school, I used to take the cows from Ballast Quay farm, down Anglesea Road, down the High Street, round by the Station Hotel, and Stacey Woods, he had a greengrocer shop, and he'd never learn! Every morning he used to put his vegetables out on the steps, and the cows used to come down and make a bee-line for his vegetables, didn't they! And his vegetables were running down the hill! He knew we were coming down at half past eight in the morning, he could have waited!

Betty Govan

Ballast Quay Farm: a small mixed farm

Most farms were small, like Ballast Quay Farm, bought by the Bowes family in 1928, who still farm there. Betty and John remember the changes since the 1940s.

It was an arable farm, arable and cows, pigs. Used to do everything by horse and cart, and ploughing the fields with horses, before we had the tractor. We used to be out cleaning mangold and sugar beet when it was starry nights and moonlit nights, working on the farm. We had a cowman, we had a horseman. And then, at different times, Dad used to get odd people in to help, a lot of the local women used to go and help pick potatoes up.

Betty Govan and cows at Ballast Quay Farm, c. 1950. (Betty Govan)

German prisoners-of-war with pitchforks at Ballast Quay Farm. (Betty Govan)

I could milk. Milk by hand, yes. I used to get up in the morning, at half past five, go over into the pits and get the cows in, and just sit down and milk them. We had butter trays where, if we got a lot of milk, we used to put it in these trays and leave it overnight, and then skim the cream off in the morning. The pigs used to have what was left. And when I was a little girl, I used to sit on my bottom, in front of the fire, and churn the butter! Churn the cream up, yes!

Betty Govan

Ballast Quay farm had about 175 acres. My father had a dairy herd here. My eldest brother done the milk round. We were producers and retailers. I sold that out and changed to beef in 1972. We had about fifty acres of arable. Wheat, barley, oats, a bit of kale, a little bit of swedes, all depends on the year and the rotation, as they go round. Father used to like to have two or three acres of early potatoes. He always supplied Ed'm Green at the local fish shop, with spuds. We have a small wood, which provided logs for the farm, it provided stakes, because with cows, you've got to have a considerable amount of cattle-proof fencing everywhere.

We had pigs, we had about eight sows at one time. Around the house too, there's always some chickens. The biggest problem is Mr Fox! I always had my own chickens as a child, a pig or a calf. My father bought some sheep for me. Well, my mother died when I was three, so some people might say he spoilt me a little bit.

When I was a child, there were five men working on this farm. A horseman, cowman, my eldest brother on the milk round, my brother Bob, and my father. Then I left school in '51, and I joined them. And by that time, the horseman had left, because we'd got tractors. My son, next door, who is on the farm with me now, he gradually worked his way in with me. I've got no other workers now. We get by, we don't make a fortune. It's a way of life, but it's a happy one.

When I left school in '51, the main tools, then, were the hand hoe and the pitchfork. Farming, today, really, is easy. I had twelve or thirteen years with the thrashing drum. Oh yes, where we used to cut the barley, we used to cut the crops with the tractor and the old binder, trail it behind, or some people call it 'stookin,' and then we used to load that, cart it to the stack, and then father would have the stack thatched. Then the thrashing drums would come in, oh dear me, what a paraphernalia! There used to be people who owned the thrashing drum, there used to be three of them come in – one man on the steam engine, and one on the drum, and a spare. I'm glad those days are gone!

John Bowes

Early tractor at Ballast Quay Farm. (Betty Govan)

Farmer's wife

When the children got older I used to go and do hoeing, feeding calves. Driving the tractor if I was needed. Whatever jobs they needed me to do, really. Pulling mangold or fodder beet, cutting cauliflowers, cabbages, picking sprouts. I used to sell cauliflowers at the door and vegetables that we grew in the garden. Now I do all the paperwork, all the letter writing, all the book-keeping. If they need me out there I go and give them a hand if they're feeding, or if they've got to get cattle in, anything. I just get a call, 'Get your wellies on! You're needed!'

Shirley Bowes

Sunnymede Farm: Specialised Farming

The neighbouring farm was bought by the Dutton family in 1931. Here Jim Dutton's father Harold developed a more specialised approach.

Harold Dutton: he had a big workforce. He used to grow fields and fields of sunflowers when we were children, and then he grew outdoor tomatoes, you imagine the labour force you have for those! He actually used a siren, a work siren there. And he had a very large herd of pigs.

John Bowes

The farm was called 'Hell's Corner' when he bought it, because it's so hot, and it's a dry area, and it's very sandy. Early on, he was doing quite a lot of seed crops. We had quite a few acres of sunflower seed – I think we had the first sunflower thresher in the country, on this farm. We had lots of Wivenhoe people with big bags tied round in the front of them, cutting all the heads off by hand, with little secateurs. There was a lot of casual labour in those days, both women and men.

Then we also grew quite a lot of outdoor tomatoes for several years, which brought in the local women mostly for picking tomatoes and tying them up, side-shooting and whatnot. The lady who was in charge of them lived just up the road here, she was more or less the forewoman. She'd muster them down the village and then bring them up. Then when I came on the farm in 1960, or '61, Dad was growing early potatoes, and then we used to go round the village with the tractor and trailer, collecting all the ladies in the morning to pick potatoes, and taking them home in the afternoon.

Then eventually we got a harvester, and when equal pay came in, we got the harvester, because (a) the cost of digging is much higher if you've got all these ladies about, and (b) the University had arrived by then, and most of them went off and worked there as cleaners, so it was a job to get ladies then.

At the moment, we're having gravel dug, but when that finishes, farming-wise, it's never going to be a viable farm as just a farm, so we do a lot of the stewardship things now and the environmental things. We've got four hectares of over-winter stubble followed by summer fallow, on which we get skylarks nesting, and English partridge. And the over-winter stubble we had about thirty meadow pipits on last winter. So we get more money from that now than we get from farming.

Jim Dutton

High Farming on the Wivenhoe Park Estate

With over 1,000 acres centred on Home Farm and Fen Farm, the Wivenhoe Park Estate was run on a much grander scale, but has been equally affected by change.

It's wonderful, because there are several people on the farm who've really spent the whole of their lives here. Brian Buckle, who used to be our foreman – his father was our horseman, and he looked after my father-in-law's hunter and, to a certain extent, my hunter as well, and he looked after the Suffolks before that.

Annabel Gooch

You lived under them
Brian started on the farm in 1947, and later became foreman and right hand man to Charles Gooch.

No, we never, didn't have no unions, no. There is the farmers' union, but there was no workers' union. No. Being a horseman, your wages were quite good. You could have belonged to the union if you went and joined, but you had no need to. You lived under

them, you was happy. Because if you started kicking up rough, the first thing you'd get is, 'Well, I'm afraid you've got to go, and leave the house.'

There were fifty-three houses, and working on this estate, the rule was when you retired, if you lived under him and lived in his cottage you could live in the cottage for the rest of your life, rent free.

The whole farm was full of animals. You had your horses, which must have been about ten or a dozen, and they bred all the estate pigs, to fatten. We had a single suckle herd, of fifty or sixty cows. It's a cow what have a calf every year, and the calf suckle from March until October, then it's took off its mother, put in the yard and fattened, and go to market the following year. The sheep were Suffolks to start with, then they ended up as the old Romney Marsh ones – the monster sheep. We had a full-time shepherd here.

The horsemen used to get there at about half past six, to give the horses a feed, brush them down, and then they'd bring them out. Suffolks. The Suffolk horse was solid and sturdy from the chest right through to the back, for pulling power. You kept breeding them well, and the brood mares used to win all the prizes at the Essex and the Tendring shows. We didn't keep stallions. They used to walk the area at the right time of the year, and then the person what walked it used to lodge with my parents.

We was all arable here, so there was three types of corn growing – oats, because you need to feed all your animals. We used to roll our own oats, for the horses and the cattle. Then you grew wheat, and you grew a lot of barley to feed your pigs. So the whole place was more or less self-supporting. We grew sugar beet. Everything done by hand. You didn't spray the sugar beet, you hoed and hoed and hoed. Then they hand hoed them: sugar beet, them days, never got any diseases.

He had his own thrashing tackle, with the steam engine, to do the thrashing in the winter. Thrashing? By God, that's a dirty job! First thing in the morning, at seven, the people arrive, because they had to come from the other farms, you want a big gang. That was a wintertime job. You'd have a whole week of nothing but thrashing, and they would set the drum and the engines up. There used to be two on the stack, the drumfeeder, two bagging the grain up, one on the chaff, and probably two stacking the straw. They wanted the straw for the pigs and the cattle. And you needed the wheat chaff to feed your bullocks and your horses. Corn and chaff made the feed up.

This end of the place didn't come very modern for a long while. Everything was still horses when I done my National Service. Then I come back out again and started working in '54, they then bought me a little T-20 Ferguson [tractor], which according to the old gaffer Gooch was equivalent to one horse. So that's when things started to get modern up a bit in 1954.

Just two people work on the farm now. On 1,100 acres. That's counting the woods and everything. But, of course, there's so much on the set-aside, and what they call 'stewardship,' isn't there, where you only farm a bit in the middle and you're paid for all that wildlife round the outside.

Brian Buckle

Landowners: The Gooch Family and Wivenhoe Park

There had been two big landowners' houses in Wivenhoe, the Hall and the Park. But the Corsellis family at Wivenhoe Hall went bankrupt in 1896, and the house was burnt down in 1926. A garden folly survives next to the Congregational church, and its park became the King George V Playing Fields. Hence by the 1930s the Gooch family at Wivenhoe Park were Wivenhoe's only gentry family. Wivenhoe Park in turn was requisitioned by troops in the Second World War, becoming a headquarters for the SAS, afterwards half-reoccupied by the family, and finally in 1962 sold to become the site for the University of Essex. The Gooch family continue to farm the estate.

The house was bought by my husband's grandfather [Charles Gooch III, d. 1937] – they were all called Charles. My grandson is Charles VII, so that's how many Charles's there have been! He bought it in 1902 and he chose this estate for the land.

The land was very good, and it is. He was a classics scholar and had a wonderful library of books – Latin and Greek – at Wivenhoe Park.

Annabel Gooch

A country gentleman

I've often wondered just how interested he [Charles III] was in farming. But it obviously was something that he wanted – to set himself up as a country gentleman, the family not having been country gentlemen before that. And I suppose that's what people did, isn't it. By this time, he'd got a family coat of arms – and all the plate and silver was crested so he obviously did things in a very very thoroughgoing way, to set himself up.

Annabel Gooch

Charles Gooch IV

My father-in-law, I knew quite well. He never went to school, he had a tutor. He was extremely musical. And when he went up to Cambridge he joined the 'Footlights' band. They went on tour to India. They played at the *Café de Paris*. And he could play any instrument, and he didn't need a bit of music either. He just understood, exactly, how to produce the sound.

He was much more of a farmer. He didn't actually drive a tractor but he was very interested in

Charles Gooch at meet of Essex and Suffolk Hounds. (Annabel Gooch)

Home Guard, commanded by Charles Gooch. (Annabel Gooch)

livestock. When I married in '61 we had pigs, sheep and cattle. We had to give up the sheep because Greenstead Estate was built. Before it was built it was just green fields. There was this policy to move people out of rather squalid areas of London, in the sixties – and they had dogs, and the dogs would run over to our side, beyond Salary Brook to where the grazing was, and very often they just murdered the sheep, just pulled them apart. So, in the end they made a decision to give up sheep.

Annabel Gooch

He flung a big party on VE Day, in the wood, the old gaffer did. He was a wonderful chap for parties, he loved parties and he loved music. He was a gentleman. Whatever he said went, the old gaffer, you see, he was a gentleman.

Brian Buckle

Country manners

Charles Gooch [IV] was a country gentleman. He didn't ever want to live in London. In fact, I hardly remember him going to London. He went to London for our wedding. He did occasionally go up and take his wife shopping. He was very amusing and had a fairly bucolic sense of humour. He was quite a domineering person. He wanted the family all to do what he wanted them to do and he wanted to control.

People around here, they used to refer to him either as 'The Colonel,' because he was colonel in the local Home Guard, or 'The Squire,' and actually, he was a typical squire. He wore country clothes, he had country manners. He wasn't smooth and sophisticated. He was tall and powerfully built but he did his own thing. He was confident and he didn't really need to follow fashion, or even to follow social behaviour. He was quite good at opening the house up for charitable functions, in that way he was very generous, and he would have the hunt ball there, and he would have all sorts of big charity parties there. Charles Gooch was a well-known local character, known for his very individual personality.

Annabel Gooch

The Hunt

Venison

The Hythe gang – a lot of unemployed old boys – they used to chase the deer in Wivenhoe Park because that was full of deer in those days, a big herd of deer, and they'd build a trap and the deer would drop in the trap and then they'd kill the deer and that was all carved up and shared out amongst the families. So we had plenty of venison! We never went hungry.

Phil Faucheux

That was all parkland, because there was a big herd of deer on there. But, of course, when the Army moved in, they either ate them, or the deer disappeared.

Brian Buckle

Master of the hunt

It was father-in-law [Charles Gooch IV] who was joint master of the Essex and Suffolk. He hunted the Essex side, although we used to go and hunt over on the Suffolk side as well, but he was in control of the Essex part of the hunt. That doesn't exist any longer because it's too urban and too dangerous to hunt in this area. The hounds were kept near Hadleigh. There was a meet every year at Wivenhoe Park and the beagles used to meet too, but again they can't really hunt around here, because of all the roads. At the meets the people would come into the hall and they'd be given drinks and sausage rolls. And it's called a 'lawn meet,' so they'd stand on the lawn outside the house.

Annabel Gooch

[My father] had to look after the old hunter, because they used to hunt three times a week, didn't they, Essex and Suffolk. Yes, when it come home, that had all got to be washed with Fairy Liquid or something, you had to get it clean, a bloody white horse!

Brian Buckle

Shooting

You see, being this is a shooting estate, you wasn't allowed to catch a rabbit. They had paid keepers, and you wasn't allowed to look at a hedge if there's a rabbit or anything in a hedge, you just shut your eyes, that was so strict to shooting.

On one of Charles Gooch's shooting days, the whole place ground to a halt that day, a shooting day. Everybody what was fit enough to walk, used to have to report down to the Keepers' Cottages, and that's where the guns used to meet. Everything stopped for shooting. Don't matter what you was doing, if you was doing a critical job the day afore, 'They're shooting tomorrow. You be there, now, at nine o'clock.' It was about every fortnight, on Tuesday. But when the old gaffer was still able-bodied, when that was Christmas shoot, he used

to send the food and the drinks down from the house for the beaters. He always had crackers! The old gaffer, you see, he was a gentleman.

Brian and Agnes Buckle

Wivenhoe Park: The House Before and After the War

Into service

I went into service at Wivenhoe Park [in 1937]. I got £1.50 a month. I got Tuesday afternoon off, and Sunday once a fortnight. The uniform was blue and white with black stockings and flat shoes for the morning, black dresses and white aprons and caps for the afternoons. My bedroom was right at the top, all us servants we all lived up at the top. The butler used to come and wake us up in the morning. We had to be down in the kitchen by 5.30, not a minute later.

It was hard work. You start off by doing all the vegetables in the kitchen, all the washing up, and then I would help the cook. The kitchen table was massive, scrubbed top. I had a huge blacklead stove to do, with great big ovens each side, I had to keep that clean. That's the only cleaning I did. The only duty I did other than that was the oil lamps. Fifty-two oil lamps, I used to have to clean them every morning, fill them up, light them up every evening and then take them and plant them all over the house, for everybody, just before dusk.

There was about twenty-three of us altogether. But I'd been there about two years when it was reduced down to about nine of us. There was the cook and me and the chauffeur-gardener, there was the nanny and two under-nurses, there was the butler and the parlourmaid, and there was four housemaids, and the handyman. We all ate in the house.

Muriel Ryder

Parties every week

The family were only Mr and Mrs Gooch and the two boys. Parties every week, any excuse for a big party, the house would be chock-a-block. They always had the hunt up there, you'd be handing them out punch in the morning before they went, there'd be cocktails when they'd come back, they'd disappear, and then they'd be back again at 8 o'clock for a five course meal. There'd be at least forty of them. We never finished up in that kitchen before 11 o'clock at night, never. But whatever they had upstairs, we had downstairs. Even when the champagne was all gone, there was always some in the kitchen for us. We had some good times there.

Muriel Ryder

Out of this world

It was a four course meal every day. You also had a very good breakfast, a big fry-up and porridge. We had a huge kitchen garden, it wasn't far from the lake, a very high wall round it – everything came off the garden. They never bought vegetables. Everything was grown. We used to make all our own ice cream. We did everything, jams, marmalades, bottled fruits. All the eggs came in off the farm. You never went short of nothing. The wine cellar was always filled up.

We always had a lot of game, we'd have deer occasionally. They had two great game larders where they hung up all the pheasants and hares that were brought in by the gamekeepers. And that cook never cooked a bird or a rabbit or a pheasant or a hare, she never cooked anything, until it was crawling with maggots. The food was out of this world. I never realised that there was such food to be had.

Muriel Ryder

Adapting post-war

I first came down here in '59. And the house had wonderful marble fireplaces, marvellous eighteenth-century plasterwork, and yet because all these houses had to be redecorated after the War by the Ministry of Defence, so they were all whitewashed. But there was something rather charming about the simplicity of all that. The furniture was marvellous. Absolutely wonderful. Some of it was Victorian and there were some extraordinary Victorian sideboards with huge, over-ornately decorated mahogany with lion paw feet and countless leaves. But the really lovely furniture was mainly Regency and Georgian.

I think after the War they didn't use the top floor at all, it was just attics and storage. Only the ground floor and the first floor were used. And then moving the kitchen up from the basement was done then, because before the War they would have had a lot more staff and they would have had it below stairs.

They had a dining room table at the bottom of the staircase. There was heating downstairs and there was heating in the master bedroom upstairs, but that's all. So my husband's bedroom was freezing! It was enormous and absolutely bitterly cold!

Annabel Gooch

House staff

They had my mother-in-law and her sister's retired nanny, who did the laundry, and they had a live-in cook and her husband was one of the gardeners. And then they had various people coming in from the village, to clean. Not all that many for such a big house. I think they entertained a lot. And there were shoots too, and shooting lunches. They would bring in extra staff at times like that.

Annabel Goochr

Selling up

Father-in-law sold the house. The Essex County Council were looking for a site for the University. He wasn't looking to sell but in the end he was persuaded to. It had become a strain to keep the house going. My husband was born in the house, and he was obviously imagining that he would live there one day and bring his family up there, so it was extremely disappointing when his father decided to sell. But it was his father's decision. He said, 'It's better for you, you'll never be able to keep this going. So it's better for the whole family if we do sell it.'

Annabel Gooch

Lord of the Manor

While in many purely rural Essex villages landowners retained their social dominance unchallenged into the mid-twentieth century, Wivenhoe was also a maritime and industrial village, and local memories of the Gooch family suggest more mixed attitudes.

I remember when old man Gooch who used to keep the Wivenhoe Park, when he died, we was at the boys' school, we was schoolchildren, and we all had to parade outside the school so we could see his coffin coming down on a wagon, with horses. The coffin was on one of the old corn wagons. That was just like a coronation that was to us in them days.

Charles Tayler

Fair shares when rabbiting

When the harvest was going to be cut by the horse-drawn reapers, word would get around who was cutting and where and then we'd tear up to the fields and wander around behind the harvester and when the rabbit bolted out everyone would chase him because it was extra meat. Meat was on ration, you couldn't get an awful lot. But it was great if you took a rabbit home. That was two days' meal, a good-sized rabbit.

But Mr Gooch who owned Wivenhoe Park, he was the fairest man that I ever met. A lot of boys are quicker at catching rabbits than others. And he would make every boy who caught a rabbit put the rabbits in line at the gate. There would be a huge line of them. And when the field had finished cutting he would allow the man who drove the binder and the man who sat on the binder to take a rabbit each. And he would get all the children to line up and take a rabbit as they went out – so one boy didn't go home with half a dozen. He was very fair, Mr Gooch.

Glendower Jackson

Lords of the manor, almost

The Gooches were the lords of the manor, almost. And, of course, Mr Gooch never missed going to church.

Freda Annis

'Goochie' was his nickname. I suppose he thought he was the Lord of the Manor, above most, and a little bit aloof. I was from the working-class and we didn't really mix.

Alan Green

'Good morning, Gooch'

Dad was working up there one day and there was Bill Clark and several of his bosses, and Dad was filling the cement thing. And Mr Gooch comes over and says, 'Good morning, Mr Clark. Good morning, Mr So-and-So.' And, 'Good morning, Gibson.' And he did not turn a hair, Dad just said, 'Good morning, Gooch.'

Sylvia Weatherall

Poverty and Unemployment

But in the 1930s Wivenhoe's industries were in trouble. Wivenhoe's upstream shipyard was not working for most of the 1920s and 1930s, and population fell from 2,400 in 1901 to 2,100 in 1931. So the old sense of social hierarchy and distance was reinforced by poverty, unemployment and poor housing, which was then concentrated in lower Wivenhoe.

Unemployment

At that time, in the thirties, the Employment Exchange was based in Alma Street, and the whole queue, every morning, right up and turn right up towards the Grosvenor pub there, there was this queue, because they had to go and sign their names every day, otherwise they didn't get the benefits. And at that particular time, things were pretty rough, and Mr Gooch, who had the whole Wivenhoe Park, gave the unemployed people permission to go and collect wood.

Now, a lot of people who were tradesmen didn't take kindly to the idea of going out and doing some other job, and I can recall as a kiddie, every day, on the top of Station Road, where the railway bridge is, there would be this collection of men, and their whole day was there, walking up and down, chatting, smoking, having a half a pint. There was, at the time, at the Co-op – up the top of the village – a reading room, where one could go and play cards and a lot of them used to go up there.

Don Smith

Hard times

When he was unemployed, my father used to cycle miles to get work. He was in the building trade then. Cycled many miles. And I do know that there were two or three shipwrights who actually used to cycle from Wivenhoe to Harwich, when they were building the Parkeston Quay. But there was hard times. I believe things got to a point where if you refused work, probably your benefits were withdrawn. A lot of them actually did work in putting the sewer on in Wivenhoe.

Don Smith

On the dole

I was out of work for a long while. And the dole was half-a-crown a week! A pig of a man used to throw it at me! Down Alma Street, it was local. You signed on and the boss used to find you jobs. The only thing he ever found me was service. So I used to go, because you had to, but I used to tell the people to put 'Unsuitable' on it and I got away with that for a while! But you could only draw dole for so long. And then I went to the clothing factory in Alma Street and never looked back.

Marjorie Goldstraw

Supplementing the diet

My dad used to kill birds and we used to eat them for our dinner. Little birds! Poor little sparrows!

There was a house that nobody lived in and my dad used to put all the bread down and over the top of it he used to put a netting, and when he got them all under there he used to knock them and kill them. And then my mother used to pluck them. But they didn't have hardly any meat or anything on it underneath!

Ivy Knappett

Shaking the empty cloth

I can remember in the 1930s, during the slump, there were terraced houses in Park Road, with the toilet right opposite, and I've known women come out and shake the cloth so that neighbours thought they'd a meal, and they hadn't. Pride, you know.

Marjorie Goldstraw

Hand-me-downs

We didn't have much new things, we had somebody's clothes. If our mothers got them cheap from somewhere we used to think they were lovely, except you met somebody and they'd say, 'Oh, the girl what's-her-name had that coat on last week.'

At school, we were stuck at the back if we had old clothes on. And then the people who'd got money, their daughters was dressed nice, they were put in the front. But if we had an old dress or anything, all of us was put at the back. Fancy doing that! So if they had visitors in, they thought that the whole school was nice, didn't they? The rich was in the front, and the poor stuck up at the back!

Ivy Knappett

Houses

Housing until the 1940s included dense old courtyards and alleys, and quayside houses like the Folly were regularly inundated by the tides: Nicholas Butler contentiously called these 'noisome, fetid places.' From this flowed social distinctions within the community, including the division into 'up-streeters' and 'down-streeters.'

There was a social distinction. There was poverty, on a small scale, mainly along the Folly, where the poorer families lived.

Tony Forsgate

Living at the end of the Folly [in the Husk House, now the only surviving part of the yard], on several occasions, we had floods. Once, it was an exceptionally big tide, and I cleared everything from downstairs. But in those days, that house was regularly flooded to a depth of two foot six, three feet. The people that lived along the Folly, they knew when there would be floods, but they took no precautions. It's just something people accepted and lived with.

Frank Hodgson

It wasn't legally mandatory then to have a cistern to flush the toilet with. Because when they put the water mains on in Wivenhoe in 1901, where you had six houses and an alley in the middle you probably had two taps in the yard. You went to the tap and you filled a bucket of water and that was your cistern. We didn't have a sink or anything in the house, but we had a toilet and an outhouse outside. There were quite a lot of these yards in Wivenhoe. In Manor Road, there was the same set-up. Unless you owned the house you never had the water inside, you had it outside.

Don Smith

When I got married, I lived right on the Quay – the houses that are pulled down now. And then from there, we went to Alma Street. And that was quite posh, in a way. Then we got into Brook Street, and that's where I finished. Oh, but everybody thought we were posh! If you got up where my mother lived, on the hill, oh, they were the hoity-toities!

My dad earned good money there [as a Wivenhoe Shipyard riveter], and my mother used to say, 'Now, don't you play with so and so down there,' no, they weren't good enough for me, you know! I'm only

talking when we got a bit better in money, but when we were poorer, she let me play with anybody!

Ivy Knappett

Up-Streeters and Down-Streeters

You've got to realise Wivenhoe has got an invisible dividing line, and that is Belle Vue Road. Now, that dividing line makes it 'up-streeters' and 'down-streeters.' It was always considered the people that lived in the up-street had the money and the people who lived down in the down-street, the older part of the village, down in the bottom, they were the poorer people. Wherever you got a game going on like cricket, football, or hockey you immediately could choose up-streets and down-streets – them versus us, so to speak.

Glendower Jackson

There was quite a gang of us. There was an 'up street' gang and a 'down street' gang. I was in the 'up street' gang. And when there was an election on we used to fight with each other. It was all sham but we used to parade with each other and that was a well-known thing.

Phil Faucheux

Later on we used to play games in the street at night – there was no television, hardly had a radio to be honest with you! We considered ourselves 'up-streeters' and 'down-streeters.' If you lived down the bottom you were 'brung'd up,' and if you lived up the top, you were 'brought up.' It was 'them' and 'us.' The down-streeters could easily form six or seven football teams. The up-streeters were limited, mainly due to the lack of houses, and class – and it was like that, I can assure you!

Peter Sainty

three

The Riverside

CK 54 Essex Girl, *skipper Ernie Vince and CK 59* Fisher Girl, *skipper Guy Downing, built for North Sea Canners 1956, at Wivenhoe c. 1960. (Nottage)*

River Traffic and the Port

The Colne at Wivenhoe has been a working river for centuries. Fishing, shipbuilding, and also less continuously the port, can all be traced back to the late middle ages. There were two ferries across to Rowhedge and Fingringhoe, and cargo boats heading up to Colchester's Hythe. Wivenhoe was also a key centre for laying up and crewing the great steam yachts, with up to forty laying downstream for early twentieth-century winters. The skipper of George V's Britannia, Captain Albert Turner, was a Wivenhoe man; Ernie Vince is the last professional ocean skipper of that era.

In the last fifty years nearly all that has gone. The regular ferries ceased with the 1953 floods, although now a summer weekend ferry has been revived by volunteers. Both shipbuilding and the port finally ended in the 1980s. A century ago there were more than 200 fishermen in Wivenhoe, today under five. With the closing of the Hythe port in 1999 you no longer see great cargo ships slip silently upstream. Today the Colne lives primarily as a pleasure river, for dinghy and cruiser sailing.

Ferries

[The Rowhedge workforce included] quite a number from Wivenhoe. Used to have to cross the ferry, the ferry went full toss at that time of the day! Used to pile in, and old Captain Jones, he used to punt across, continually. Because it would be a race in the morning, coming down right across the marsh and from the station, and again at night, coming out of the Yard to get home to Wivenhoe, you all raced down to the ferry to see if you could get on board first! He could only take about a dozen blokes at one time!

Bill Webb

When I was at work at Cooks's, also we [were fishing for] shrimps. I'd take them across on the bike. Then dad'd come along later, and sell them in Rowhedge. He used to occasionally, if that was getting bad here, he weren't selling much here, he would go down to Rowhedge to try and sell some fish, to make a living. But basically that was for the shrimps.

Barry Green

Uncle Fred's milk all came over the ferry, from a farmer in Fingringhoe, so the farmer come down and dumped a couple of churns on the ferry hard and we'd go over and get them. If Uncle Charlie [Sainty] was indoors I'd just jump in the boat and go and get them if I was on the Quay! And then help Fred push them up to the shop. Low water spring tides, you could walk across the ferry at Wivenhoe, with thigh boots on. If that was low water/springs, then he would drive the cart through the river and take the churns up the shop, and go back again while the tide was down.

Ernie Vince

We used to go from Wivenhoe Ferry over to Fingringhoe. We used to walk right round Fingringhoe to the Whalebone, the pub there, and then walk back to Rowhedge, to the Albion, and get a ferry back. Because we used to pick blackberries when we were kids, over on the pits where Dene Park is built now, and we used to walk all the way over to Rowhedge to sell these blackberries! We did it for years, and the money we got, which was a penny or tuppence, we used to save that to go to our Sunday school outing at Walton with the church Sunday school.

Betty Govan

Sailing barges

The barges used to come up. Oh, they were beautiful! The stackies, with the straw. It used to be stacked up so high! And there was only just that little bit of the boat above the waterline, wonderful old boats. We used to sit on the Quay, 'Oh, here come the barges.' And three or four would come up at a time. They were taking the straw to the Hythe. The Hythe was a fascinating place in those days, there were great big granaries. There was one man, used to cycle down to the 'Third Stile,' and then the barge would come up that far, just past the iron bridge, one of the men would come over in a boat and he would pilot it up the river. It was difficult to know the landmarks. Well, there was so much silt. They used to have a boat at the Hythe, the mud dredger, to take it up and then dump it on the marshes.

Freda Annis

Thames barges used to sail up to Colchester and they would quite often tack up here past Wivenhoe, and a number of times I'd be out in the yard, and stand on the rail there, and just watch them tack. They were brilliant, those skippers. They could come across that river, and they could tack, and the stern would come round like that, and miss us by a hair's breadth! Brilliant!

Bill Webb

The Port

There had been several quays and warehouses in Wivenhoe in the past, and fish is still being landed. From 1966, however, Gliksten's – later Meredith's – operated a much larger scale timber port on the site of the former Wivenhoe Shipyard. This was succeeded in 1981 by the general purpose Wivenhoe Port Ltd, which was to close after considerable friction in 1988.

Meredith's, which was the timber company, which was importing/exporting timber, sold up and moved down to Tilbury. So Dave Watts went to have a look at it, and he and his brother Danny bought it. I came across with Dave, to help set the new company up. So they changed it to a general cargo port, import/export.

So we bought the Port in '81, and with great excitement the first ship came in. And in its heyday, we probably brought in half a million tons of cargoes. We built a weighbridge, and we built new

warehousing with grain walling in, so we could store bulk cargoes, and later on, we built a big warehouse down on the marsh. The cargoes came mainly from Rotterdam – trans-shipment cargoes. We used to bring stuff round from the Thames, as well, in the early days – small barges with cargoes of all sorts. On the import side, various types of grain, coal, timber, fertilisers, bricks, steel. And we brought in timber and steel from Poland and Scandinavia.

We had a workforce of about twenty We didn't stop them but we were always proud of the fact that none of our employees ever felt the need to have the protection of the Union behind them, because Dave was of a view that he would look after the staff, and he did. And they were happy with their lot – as we all were. It was a very happy time, apart from all the controversy that went on. The actual working environment, and the very family feeling that was generated amongst the workforce, was a really great time.

Pat Alston

The end of the port

After the Dock Labour Scheme was broken the other ports were able to be more flexible in what they could handle, and dictate more to their stevedores what they would work and what they wouldn't work. So they became more competitive and places like Ipswich and Tilbury could handle bigger ships. We started to see a downturn in trade and it was becoming more difficult to get cargoes, so eventually we came down to almost an either/or situation for the local people. Either we can build further down so that we can have more cargoes of a type which aren't very friendly, but if not, then let's use the land for something else. Let's build houses on it. And even that went to a Public Inquiry, but ultimately, it came down in favour of building the houses.

I remember baking a cake, and putting, 'Farewell Wivenhoe Port'! We commissioned that picture from Mike Heard, local artist. Dave has got the original and we had 40 limited edition prints made which he's numbered and personally signed, and that was given to each of the employees and some of our customers as a goodbye and thank you, and something to remember it by.

Pat Alston

The Nottage

The Nottage was formed in 1896, as a result of a bequest by [an army] captain, Charles Nottage, who was a Victorian gentleman yachtsman. It was set up in what we now call the Lucy Dee, which is next to the Black Buoy, and it was there from 1896 till 1947, and then it outgrew the place, and Hector Barr, who built where we are now, as a sail loft, decided to pack up, and the trustees bought the place off him.

Mike Downes

Really, the waterside was still run, in the late 1960s, very largely by the local 'squirearchy' – known to some of the downstreeters as the 'mafia'. You were either part of the very small upper Wivenhoe squire-archy or mafiosi or you weren't! And the mafiosi did, very much, keep everything to themselves, and they wanted things run just their own way. For instance, the mud berths in front of the Nottage appeared to be let out on a favour basis, 'You can put your boat in there, and don't forget, you can come and do a little job for me.' This style of thing.

There wasn't much that went on at the Nottage Institute. In the winter, they had a few short talks, just for invited audiences. There was a boat-building class run by Billy Woods, a local shipwright, but only about four or five boats were under build at one time and they took years to complete. There was a very long waiting list, and ladies were definitely not enrolled. And they were doing non-certificated navigation courses. The Nottage was rarely open to the public.

But behind the scenes, things were happening. In November 1971, the trustees recognised a crisis: 'Money's running out. Something's got to be done to save the place, otherwise we'll literally have to think about closing down.' Trust income

Boatbuilding class at the Nottage Institute. (Nottage)

was pretty static but expenses were raising steadily. The money coming in was staying fairly static, but rates and everything else were going up. They were also paying the instructors, but all the classes were completely free of charge. Things were in a pickle and the outlook was grim.

I'd only been retired a matter of weeks when I was suddenly approached, and in an extremely short time became the treasurer and secretary. I have to say, we were rather staggered by what we found! We immediately saw that income was by no ways matching expenditure. There was no book-keeping system at all, to my surprise! Coming from a fairly well-ordered life [in the City], I thought this was a bit odd! And I thought, 'Well, this really can't go on!'

I wrote a report setting out how it would be a terrible shame for the Nottage, after all those years, to close down, and that all that was needed was to start running some classes on a 'semi-commercial basis.' These 'commercial' ideas were not exactly enthusiastically received, but after quite a struggle fee-paying classes did begin. Cdr Peter Hunnaball started the whole Royal Yachting Association G15 Syllabus, and there were other classes including meteorology, ropeworking, engine maintenance, first aid, all sorts of things. Course fees were at a very cheap rate and the courses were actively marketed, so soon over 200 students were attending the winter courses. We used to go round each year, in our motor car, covering an area from Felixstowe to Maldon, to all the sailing clubs. It was all yachtsmen, who were coming to the classes, and it really did take off in a big way.

By this time, we – my wife Georgina and I – were running the Friends of the Nottage Association, formed in 1972, but we met with a disaster, because some 150 people turned up for a talk about the barquentine *Cap Pilar* and her voyage round the world, given by her bo'sun John Donnelly. And in the interval, the floor gave way under the weight of the people! Also fire precautions were rudimentary; if you needed to evacuate quickly, the only way you get down was to slide down on a rope! So, then, in 1975-7, a big programme was started: the walls were strengthened, new toilets, a little galley, the stairs were moved, and a balcony built on the front.

By this time we'd got ladies coming. Oh, it was a great step forward! And the museum side began to build up. Michael Dunn and Georgina began a major conservation programme on the pictures and artefacts at the Nottage. We started getting the children to come, regular visits from the local schools.

The other thing which baffled us was that no one seemed to know much at all about the history of the Nottage. They knew you weren't allowed to have on the premises round there, any books of a religious nature. You could have no parson, priest, ayatollah or anybody else of a religious faction as a committee member. But when I asked, nobody had the faintest idea. The only thing they did seem to know was that Charles George Nottage's father had been a lord mayor of London. And unfortunately, the Trustees had had a copy of the will, but lost it! There is no trust deed, the Nottage is run under part of the actual will. After a lot of research I traced and met Muriel Spink, the daughter of Charles, who lived in Monte Carlo – resulting in much interesting information.

Bill Ellis

Now in the wintertime we run evening classes and weekend courses, mainly for yachtsmen. Through the 'Friends of the Nottage' we run a winter series of lectures, not all nautical subjects, on various subjects, and also a film club.

The boat-building is done downstairs, that's been going quite a few years now. It's now run by a boat-builder from Rowhedge, called Fabian Bush, and we take between nine and eleven or so students. It takes about 400-450 hours to build a Nottage dinghy, so it's usually spaced at least over four to five years. We're totally self-supporting. No grants, nothing, no. It's always touch and go. We have to adjust our course fees.

Mike Downes

Fishing

Catches of sole, brill and herrings go back in the records to 1481 and these are fish still to be had in the Thames Estuary. The transformation of local fishing is less due to changing fish stocks than to increases in catching power and most recently to quotas.

You could go down on the Quay, the poor, and they'd give you a 'bend' – a wire, a ring, with these little dabs and small plaice strung on them – and just throw them on the Quay for people to pick up, and it was really fresh. And lovely shrimps too.

Marjorie Goldstraw

Three Fishermen

Ken Green

Ken's Uncle Ernie had the family fishing boat, a big motorised bawley, the Volunteer, *Uncle Edwin had the fish and chip shop in Wivenhoe, and his father sold fish*

CK 299 Elise, *in smack race, with skipper Friday Green, 1914. (Peter Green)*

and shrimps in Colchester. Ken was a fisherman himself in 1949-51, and then from 1953 selling and smoking fish, in Colchester and later in Wivenhoe.

Fishing: a family affair

This was a very important pink shrimp area, centred really on Harwich, it was shrimps in the summer and spratting in the winter. After the War, there'd been a golden period, because the fish had been left alone, and the shrimps had multiplied. So Uncle Ernie, and Boxer Pike his crew, they would go to sea on a daily basis. They would start fishing about one or two o'clock in the morning, and land about one or two o'clock midday. Then my father would pick the shrimps up, and he would go and sell them in Colchester in the afternoon, as did Uncle Edwin down here, at the fish shop. So it was very much a family affair.

I left school in 1949, I was itching to get to sea, and so at fifteen I went to sea with Uncle Ernie and Boxer Pike, and I was very much the lowest form of animal life on board, I can tell you!

The first week that we fished, we were shrimping, and we'd pulled down on the first haul, and the net had got badly torn, so it had to be mended, a bit of a bodge-up to get it ready to shoot away the next haul. So I was given the job of steering the boat. And at fifteen, and not very big either – I was only 5 feet 4 inches when I left school! – I'd got this huge tiller. The wind was just off the bow, and a lot of swell, which made the boat not only pitch, but roll as well, so it was wriggling, which made the tiller swing side to side, quite violently, and as I stood up to get hold of the tiller, so it knocked me down again! After about three or four times of that, I decided the only thing I could do was to lay on top of it and just get my arms round it, and just hold on!

At sixteen, I was the ship's cook, and my goodness me, how I didn't poison people I don't know! Wintertime, you were liable to be away one day, but you might be away for a week or a fortnight, if you were over the other side of the Estuary and got stormbound. So I was the cook, and on one occasion, we used to make a 'duff' – flour and water, and put it in a bag and boil it up – but if you didn't put a plate in the bottom of the saucepan, it stuck to the bottom. You had gravy with it for the first course, and jam with it for the second course! And I remember Uncle Ernest saying, 'Oh, I like it burnt,' he said, 'I'll have that.' I said, 'Jolly good, you can have the cloth with it, because that's stuck to it!'

Golden Dawn

I came away from the family business in the early seventies, to go out on my own, because I wanted to get back to fishing boats again. We decided to buy a trawler of our own, *Golden Dawn*. We got Ernie Vince, who was a local skipper, lined up for that job. He was skippering a sand barge, the *Bert Prior*, which still comes up to Fingringhoe. And that worked for us for a long time, the *Golden*

Dawn. She provided us with a lot of local fish, which we either sold at the shop, or we marketed ourselves, wholesale. And, it gave us the impetus, because people – and try as we might to tell them different – they really wanted to believe that we caught all our own fish! Which wasn't possible because, of course, you don't catch haddocks in these waters, for instance! But that gave a very good impression of us, and, yes, we did very well. I don't suppose, if we'd isolated *Golden Dawn*, she actually operated very profitably but in the fullness of the whole business, she was very very good for us.

But she did come unstuck when she was moored in Brightlingsea, and she was hit by a sand barge

Right: *Ken Green and his Uncle Ernie aboard, 1950.* (Ken Green)

Below: *CK 299* Mariner, *skipper Richard Jacobs, in a race at Southend, 1980.* (Nottage)

when she was moored. It was a hit-and-run job, and nobody would put their hand up to doing it. There was a wall of silence. It took three years to actually prove who'd done it. When I went around Brightlingsea to get evidence, talking to people, nobody knew anything, nobody saw anything, nobody heard anything, nobody knew anything. So *Golden Dawn* had to be hauled out, and she was repaired at Cooks, and she was very badly damaged. But she did get back to sea again. I suppose she was eight to ten years fishing.

Hands on the factory floor

In the 1970s I started wholesaling and retailing, and curing, in West Street here, yes, with two smaller kilns I had down here. I was here working about twenty-eight years. Time slips away so quick when you're enjoying yourself, doesn't it! Even today, I still enjoy the job, I've been filleting fish today, and I enjoy it. I want to be actually processing and smoking and filleting, and actually hands on, on the factory floor.

Fish stocks: not all gloom and doom

With the fish stocks, change is the word. It's not all gloom and doom. The cockle fishery is a success. Last year, locally we had a very good cod fishery. But the predominant fishery now, in the Thames Estuary is sole fishing, that's what most of the boats are going for at this present moment, sole and skate.

Everybody has a different theory on the shrimps, but I think it's a natural factor. It may well be that trawling for shrimps has destroyed the habitat of the shrimps, because they used to produce a very fragile rawse, like honeycomb, that they used to live in – the feed for the shrimps. I think that fishing probably didn't do any good to that habitat. Yet it still goes on in the Wash. We get cod now, where we didn't used to get them years ago. There was a good sprat fishery off Lowestoft this year, and they came as close as Harwich. So, no, the sprats haven't disappeared. And we do have a local herring fishery as well.

The smaller fish are shoaling fish, and they don't always do the same thing year in and year out. Water temperature is very important. Sometimes the sprat shoals don't come into the Thames Estuary, which they'd always done years ago. Now they are spasmodic, and sometimes they hardly appear at all in the wintertime.

Hunting in the wild

These days, a lot of fish species are under threat because they don't stand much of a chance now. We know too much about their habits, we have too many methods of detecting where they are, and everybody, of course, still has the same attitude of 'Fill your boots while you've got the chance.' So that's what happens, even when people are supposed to be working to quotas. Getting fishermen under control is not natural, because it still is a hunting in the wild process. It's a very difficult job to police and to sort out.

I'm a supreme optimist, and there aren't many like me in the fish trade. It's always tended to be a gloom and doom trade! I'm not, by that, saying things are good at the present moment, because they're difficult, very difficult. But I think it will always survive, yes. I think, while people have got the inkling to go to sea, then I think it will survive.

Brian Green

Brian Green fished from 1947, starting in his father's bawley, the Alice Matilda, *and continuing until his father died in 1965. Brian is Ken's cousin.*

My father, after the latter part of the War, did go fishing. I used to crave to go with him – and this was while I was at school – and eventually he let me go one day, snitched a day from school, and although I felt sick, I still wanted to go again!

Skipper Bill Woodward of the Christine *sieving shrimps. (Nottage)*

Stowboating

Fifteen when I started fishing, that was 1947. And that was as primitive as you could get. It was in the winter, it was the November, and we were spratting – no electrical device to find fish with then – you used to watch for a flock of seagulls, and they told you they was working over sprats. You had the old 'stowboat gear,' for which you had to lay at anchor, and you couldn't get your nets back until the tide eased, because there was so much tide you couldn't get them up. Stowboating gear, that's a big net, about 200 foot long, and that's supported by two poles in the front. The top one is held on to the boat, and the bottom one drops on its own weight, with a railway sleeper stuck to it for weight. And then a square-fronted net streams out for about 200 feet behind the boat and underneath it, hoping that the shoal of sprats are going to go into it. And quite often they did. You'd get twelve, fourteen ton of sprats would go into that net if you were in the way of the shoal properly.

Tie me to the tiller

You hauled all [the gear] up on a windlass with spikes. There was a little winch aboard, but that wasn't [used for] much more than pulling the anchor up. But there was no wheelhouse. My father used to put a rope round me and tie me to the tiller, so if I fell over, he could pull me back on the bit of rope!

Laying out there at night

The navigation lights were oil, so there was no power from those. And we laid there at night, and all the ships, then, from the Thames, come sliding past so close, they nearly swamped you. I could hit them with a piece of coal! That's how close they were.

Rodney Bowes

Grandson of Ernie Vince, son of John Bowes, born 1960, Rodney grew up on Ballast Quay Farm, but decided to become a fisherman, and at sixteen went to Lowestoft Maritime College. He bought his own shrimp trawler, Fanny Ann.

My grandfather Ernie had been at sea, on and off, all his life. I don't know if that's a little bit of him in me. And my cousin [John Bowes] had a fishing boat and worked out of Wivenhoe, and weekends and summer holidays, if we weren't on the farm, we were out fishing with him. That's where I got the bug, and then never got over it – not yet, anyway!

Knowing the Thames

Starting off was a bit of a bloody nightmare! A big learning curve. That was just lack of knowledge. In the Thames, it's a little bit different today, but you need experience, and the only way to gain experience is to spend a lot of time with other people, and then, *then*, they didn't divulge any sort of valuable information regarding where the wrecks were, or what type of ground you were fishing on.

Because the Thames is littered with wreckage, mostly from the Second World War – aeroplanes, some shipping, mines, bombs. There's more wreckage in the Thames Estuary than anywhere in the rest of the country. They cost you a lot of time and money, if you lose a net and a set of otter boards.

No big secrets any more

There's no big secrets any more, the last few years, it's probably ninety per cent of the fishermen have got track plotters now, so everything's kept on a disk or on a tape. The more modern ones are all video, you can zoom in, zoom out, you could be working a small piece of ground, and on your screen, you can zoom in. And I think people generally do get on better than they did. There's still a lot of competition, but when my grandfather was fishing, in his day, crews used to get told off just for looking at another boat as they went by, never mind speaking to them! Totally different world!

Worms and butterfish

Most of the fish we fish for, with the exception of herrings, you don't see on an echo sounder, so it's just a case of knowing the seasons and knowing where the feed is. There's worms, and 'butterfish' – which are a little shellfish about the size of your little fingernail, that come out the ground – they appear in about June and go through till September, and then they disappear again. But sole love them – which is what we fish for mostly. If you know where the little trails of those are, which are not much wider than the width of a road, over the years you get, hopefully, you get to find out these little things. If you find the feed, you find the fish, normally. A lot of them are, literally, half a mile long by the width of the road out here, and if there's not too many boats about you can farm your bits, leave it alone for a day or two, and there'll be fish come back, the fish'll keep coming back if there's feed there.

Poor winters

I sometimes used to fish in the river here for shrimps, brown shrimps, and the last two or three years I've gone down to Boston, Lincolnshire, trawling for brown shrimps in the winter. But the winters, the last few years, have got so there's very little to do here. Herring, there's very little demand for herrings. I don't know whether that's the size of the ones we get here, or it's only the older generation know how to eat them.

Quotas for a rowing boat

The quota system, that sickens me. Now 80 per cent of the British Dover sole quota and 80 per cent of the British plaice quota is in the hands of Dutch fishing vessels. For our quota allocations, they started off with very little, and that just got less and less and less. They were on a pathetic amount of fish. Really you wouldn't run a rowing boat on what they were allowed to catch. So they did what anybody else would do, they had to fiddle to survive.

The bigger boats have gone. I think there's more smaller ones, although they're gradually withering away. And there's no youngsters to come into the job either. So anybody who has it after I'm gone, if there's any fish to catch, they won't have a lot of competition.

Every day is different

Once you've got the bug – I don't know whether that's the freedom of it, we work all silly hours because of the tides, and my wife will ask me what I'm doing tomorrow, the next day, I never know, I've had twenty-four years but can't give her a straight answer. You don't know, you don't know whether the weather's going to be all right or not. Every day is different. And I think that's quite rare, to really enjoy what you do. Every day is a challenge. I'm at my happiest when I'm at work, to be honest!

The Shipyards

Wivenhoe had been famous in the mid-nineteenth century for the building of ocean racing yachts by Sainty and Harvey. Apart from smaller boat-builders there were two main shipyards. The upstream yard by the railway station was taken over in 1888 by Forrestt's from Limehouse, who constructed the dry dock and built a great variety of steel ships, employing a workforce of some 300 until their bankruptcy in 1922. To make matters worse, in 1936 the big shipbuilding companies obtained legislation banning small shipyards from steel boat-building for forty years. But with the sudden demands of the War the yard was reopened as the Wivenhoe Shipyard from 1939 until 1961 for naval work, but managed by the Rowhedge shipyard. It then became the site for Wivenhoe Port.

At the downstream yard James Husk built small smacks and yachts from the 1840s until 1937. This yard was also reopened in the War, by Vospers of Portsmouth, building motor torpedo boats from 1940 until 1946. They were finally succeeded by James W. Cook & Co (Wivenhoe) Ltd, who built many types of craft – coasters, dredgers, tugs, pilot boats and lighters – launching over twenty a year in the 1960s. They continued to build boats, less profitably, until their liquidation and closure in 1986. One of their last boats was the three-masted ocean sailing ship, the Lord Nelson.

That noise!

My grandfather was a riveter. My father had to be at work at half past seven in the morning. He always walked to the Rowhedge Ferry, because before the War, Wivenhoe Shipyard was not in operation, so the shipyard workers all went over to Rowhedge.

Then with the War it was a thriving place then! When the hooter went at half past twelve, the High Street was full of bikes, with the men coming home to lunch. And there was always the noise of the shipyards, the banging. It wasn't so much the noise of riveters, they were soon taken over by the welders, but there was always banging going on. It was just something that accompanied life – that noise.

Olive Whaley

Controlled by the hooters

Wivenhoe was controlled by the hooters in the two shipyards. The hooter went at five and twenty past seven, and again at half past seven in the morning. It was a loud hooter, you could hear it up at the Park Hotel.

We started at 7.30 a.m. – on the dot. Tight. You were allowed three minutes, and if you didn't make the three minutes, the clock was closed, you didn't get in till nine o'clock.

John Bines

Upstream Yard

Bare grass and weeds

After the First World War, there was a demise of shipbuilding, and this yard here, more or less closed. As a young boy, living down at the bottom of the village, wandering around, I can remember them building a small tug. Only one. I used to look through the knot-holes in the wooden fences, see what was there. But the industry went even further and further downhill. There was a big sale. They sold everything. Even took the railway lines up. The whole thing was stripped and just left bare grass and weeds.

Don Smith

American equipment

Eventually, in 1951 I came back to the Wivenhoe Shipyard, and I was there ten years until the last day when it closed. They'd just started to build these new 'ton' class minesweepers, and the workforce must have reached in excess of 100. I just lapped it up, loved it!

I'd progressed from being a complete turner, to a turner/fitter, so I was working more with my hands, on a bench, and the installation of machinery on the ships, and that was quite a complex job to do, for a little shipyard. We had new equipment come in, and it was all American. I presume it was a lease/lend deal, providing equipment. During the War, every hand tool, drill, was all electric, in that yard. After this, everything was pneumatic. Now, pneumatic hand tools are much safer. With an electric drill, drilling into wet wood, if that got jammed up, you couldn't hold it, unless you switched it off. If you couldn't switch it off, it would take you. Now, a pneumatic drill has a safety valve on it, so you can't get a shock. So all that equipment for this new contract, came from America.

Don Smith

Thousands of bolts

The 'ton' class minesweepers, they weren't steel, they were aluminium [frames] with mahogany [skins], and there was rivets, all riveting went on, for the hulls. They were double-skinned, they had one plank of an inch, and one plank of two inches thick, right the way round, and they were all bolted on. They were all bolted on. Thousands of bolts! And every little bolt head went in, and then a little, like, plug, was put over the top. There was a very strict control on the amount of magnetic material in them, so the anchors were all bronze, the anchor chain was all bronze. For a small ship, I believe they cost about three quarters of a million pounds each. They're now all fibre-glass, what they have now.

But the yard came to the close after they built these three. Then they built four small boats for the Navy, which were called 'provision tenders,' and they were only about fifty feet long, and they were the four last ones.

Don Smith

Minesweeper in Wivenhoe Shipyard dry dock, c. 1946-8. (Glendower Jackson 27)

A brilliant plater

In the 1950s, you picked it up as you went along. You worked with another plater, you see. You worked with another plater, and you learnt it as you went along. I picked up with man in the village called Charlie Sainty, he was a marvellous plater. One of the best platers on this coast for miles, that man. Brilliant man. I worked with him for a long while, I learnt a lot off of him. Cooks's had a strike over him, at one time! Well, he was doing a job, and he done it the way he wanted to do it, and the management didn't like it, and wanted him to change it. And he said, 'No, I'm doing it my way.' They wouldn't give in to him, so all the men walked out on strike.

Charlie wanted to work outside in the open, and that's where he done it. He finished his job there, and then the crane lifted it all up in one big piece. That was part of the bows. Well when they could see what he was doing, they more or less apologised and said he was right. You know, he *was* right.

Charles Sansom

The union

Oh yes, you had to obey the strike. You had to come out whether you wanted to come out or not. They used to hold the union meetings, the boilermakers, in the Station Hotel, up in the top, and he used to live in this village, the founder of the boilermakers – Ted Hill. He used to go to work on the train every day, in his Homburg hat, and coat. Oh yes!

We never thought much of the shipwrights, and they didn't think much of the iron workers! That was like that all the way through. 'Oh, this is our job.' Oh, chalk line stuff. But no, it wasn't harmful to anybody, just niggling between one another.

Charles Sansom

An excuse to have a party

When Wivenhoe Shipyard opened in '39, Mr Frank Butcher, who was the managing director of Rowhedge, had a friend, by the name of Mr Robert Buckingham, who had no knowledge, whatsoever, of shipbuilding, but he was a businessman. And he was put over here as the Managing Director – always a bit of a Churchillian sort of man, with a big cigar, and a big trilby hat, and a white moustache. He was a great one for a social life, and even though we had a war on our hands, with terrible things happening, the launching of a minesweeper, for him, was an excuse to have a party. He would invite lots of people from the military in the area, and they had these photographs taken. We, at the Nottage, have got dozens of photographs of Robert Buckingham!

Don Smith

Downstream Yard

In 1940 the smaller downstream boatyard was taken over by the Admiralty, and a complete new building called a 'shadow factory' was built, and that was for the production of motor torpedo boats, for Vospers at Portsmouth, because they'd been blitzed completely. They went [succeeded], eventually, by James W. Cook's, and I went there as a fitter in 1947.

Don Smith

Boilermakers and shipwrights

There was overtime every weekend. There was a lot of work to be done. All the boilermakers, who are steel people, plating and repairs, always had their work done on contract. In shipbuilding, boilermakers took a more aggressive stance on their work conditions and their pay. They always earned more money than engineers and shipwrights and joiners. The Boilermakers Union was very, very strong. Shipwrights not strong, though I was there just three, four years, and towards the end I did have opportunities to have contracts. I was making things on the lathes, and I would have the drawings, and you would submit your price.

Don Smith

Above: *Building small wooden boats, James Husk's Yard, c. 1935. (Nottage)*

Left: *Wooden hull, Husk's Yard, c. 1935. (Nottage)*

Opposite above: *Taking a break at Cook's: including John Bines, Peter Cole, Kenn Dadds, Ivor Gunn, Michael Durrell. (John Bines)*

Opposite below: *At Cook's building the* Lord Nelson, *140 ton square-rigged schooner for Jubilee Trust, 1985; Jack Taylor, plater. (Don Smith)*

Anglesmith

In 1948 I started with an anglesmith, Harry Pike, and I was with him all the time. We used to furnace the frames for the barges, furnace them, pull them out and bend them. I had to pull these bars out, and keep the thing hot. Everything had to be got hot. You had a furnace there, and you had to pull them out, and work quick on them, otherwise they soon cooled off. They were big coke fires, very primitive. Very primitive.

Charles Sansom

Plater's apprentice

When I started in 1957, they were just finishing the riveting days, and just going on to the fully welded boats. They were just riveting in the frames, and welding up the butts and the seams. A shipyard apprenticeship was hard in them days. I didn't do nothing, I should think for a year or more, just stood and watched, fetch and carry. Very strict union in them days. One man, one job. And if you didn't get in the union, you wouldn't get an apprenticeship.

Platers were taking the dimensions off the drawing, marking out all the plates, and then erecting them, actually building the ship, but not welding it. The draughtsmen gave them templates from the loft, and then they drew it, took it off the paper, the drawings, and then made the moulds. You just had a batten with marks on it, and you'd have a centre line, and you'd work it out from that and your drawing. And then your job was to transfer that on to the steel, on to the metal, yes. And then cut it out. And put it on the boat, and erect it. They cut with oxyacetylene. They did have, in the early days, a cutter, but they did away with that in the end, and we done everything by burning it out.

Barry Green

Plater's boy

I wanted to be a welder, but [in 1948] I got put with a plater called Cliffie Barker, very very nice man, and he talked to me, and the others got on to me, 'Oh, you don't want to be a welder! That's a riveter with his brains blown out!' So I became a plater. It was cold in the winter. All the platers had a little five-gallon drum with holes knocked in it, and had a fire. Apprenticeship's job to get that fire going and keep it going all day, you've got to keep your plater warm.

The labourers always got an earful if they didn't move the bar smoothly enough, or that stopped. No, you got your ear bashed, or your arse kicked, or hit with a two-foot rule, it was nothing to see boys and labourers get smacked because they were perfectionists, these old boys, it had to be right, and it had to look right. There was nothing to get your arms punched. Or they would get your arm between the first two fingers and nip it and twist it, and that really hurt. So you were always going to do as you were told.

John Bines

The Union

You were advised, more or less forced, into joining the Boilermakers' Union, from an age of sixteen. Because when you got to twenty-one, and you became a plater, you couldn't work anywhere if you weren't a member of the union. If you were off sick, you got five shillings a week. Not a lot, but it did help, because a lot of people got injuries, especially around the arms and their hands. It was a bit of a ritual, joining the union, you had to swear allegiance to the union.

John Bines

Shell platers, riveters and heaters

I did about a year with Cliffie. Then I moved on to shell plating. That was building and shelling up the boats, putting the hull on the boats. A shell plater was *the* top plater. There was no calculators in them days, everything was figures – an inch and three-eighths, and an inch and three-quarters – so your mental arithmetic, to be a plater, had to be good.

It was still riveting, although that was gradually moving on from when I started work. Welding was cheaper to do than riveters. The riveters involved three men in a squad – a heater, a holder up, and a riveter. It was hard work for a riveter. He'd got to put either 950, or 1,000 rivets in, to earn his week's pay, and after that it was ten bob a hundred.

The Company paid the heater. He was lowest of the low! I've seen rivet heaters cry. They had a terrible life. Rivet heaters were in at seven o'clock in the morning, get the fire going, get the first set of rivets hot. He was staring into a fire all day long. It was the worst job, that one, because the sheer noise, and what happened to riveters and holder ups was horrendous. It was just constant noise, noisy and dirty.

At one time, they had thirteen, fourteen squads of riveters in Cooks's. The riveter was using a mechanical gun, which weighed 10lbs, the gun itself, and holding a 10lb gun up for nine hours a day, with a 100lb airline, so the pressure was 100lb push, which you've got to keep… the muscles and the veins used to stick out on their arms. They were solid. And their knees, when they were under the bottom of the ship, they used to have blocks that they could put their foot on, so their knee always took the weight of that machine. They were jammed under there, had a hat on, so that their head used to be jammed up under the bottom of the boat all the time. Yes, I was glad I was a plater!

John Bines

The scree board

The dimensions were given by drawings. All the shapes were on a 'scree board,' which was a huge board in the shop, on the loft floor, so you had the shape of every plate, every frame in the ship. The

Launching MSC Volant, early 1970s. (John Bines)

seams were marked, so you knew exactly where the seams were going to be. It looked odd when you were standing looking at the scree board, because the seam on a boat was a nice straight pleasing line, but when you looked at it on the scree board, it went into lots of zig-zags! The loft floor was where the ship was laid out completely in chalk. Full-size pattern, and you weren't allowed on that floor. It was all done in chalk, so you had to be very very careful about where you walked or where you trod.

John Bines

Launching

It was always a brilliant day, launching. We all got a day off school. They used to be virtually right up to the ship, standing there within, say, ten feet of the ship, when it was going down the slipway. You wouldn't be allowed to do that today. And there was always a good party for the owners and senior representatives of the yard. Even that changed in the latter part, a certain percentage of the workmen were invited to the lunch, but normally, normally, we got a pint of beer.

John Bines

Longest serving man

I was the longest serving man, bar one. Thirty-six years. I was a plater all that time. The latter days were a lot better. Conditions had got better, you got better clothing, you got more protection, the unions played a different part, not so much of 'them and us,' as a bit more of 'Right, we'll come in with you, because you're giving our men better facilities.' There was more negotiation, more pleasant nego-tiations, rather than – really harsh; old man Charlie Newton locked us out a couple of times.

John Bines

The end of the yard

I first felt things were not going well, when George Smith went. He was the driving force of the company. He was a brilliant man, and a nice man, probably one of the best governors anybody could work for. He understood, socially, what everybody wanted. He did provide a very good wage, and very good working conditions. And he also got some good jobs as well. He wouldn't have entertained the *Zebu Express* and the *Buffalo Express*. They were really the downfall. They were too big for us, really and truly. The banks didn't give you enough time and money.

We all knew it was coming, from May, when the big pay off came. There were orders there, although we were closing. But gradually people were being paid off each week. I had the awful job, as the Shop steward, of wandering round and giving people their little brown envelopes. Then towards the end, the last boat was finished, and six or seven of us left. So we've got close on 100 years shipbuilding experience going down the river.

I worked up to the last day, which was the 6th September 1986 – it always sticks in my memory, that date. Yes, I locked up and threw the keys in the box. Jack Taylor, who was the foreman at the time, said, 'I'm not going to do that.' So I went to see the accountants who were overseeing the closure, and said to him, 'What about when we finish? Do we clear all the gear up?' 'No, no. Just leave it. Where you leave it, just drop it. Just lock up and bring the keys into the office and put them on the desk.' So I locked the door and put the keys on his office desk! Threw them in the box, and walked away.

John Bines

four

Factories, Shops, and Pubs

Co-op delivery boy Ted Harvey, 1950s. (John Stewart)

Canning, Clothing Factories and the Pit

Small maritime manufactories such as sail-making and rope-making had flourished in Wivenhoe since the eighteenth century, and more recently small engineering workshops. But from the 1930s until the 1950s, later petering out, the most notable small factories, all mainly employing women, were in canning and clothing. North Sea Canners was started by Lewis Worsp in 1932, and later became part of Wilkins of Tiptree; while the Colchester Manufacturing Company started its Alma Street clothing factory in 1935.

North Sea Canners

Money and muck

Picking out sprats was my first job, on the Quay. At about fourteen! There might have been about twelve of us was there. Well, if the high tide was 12 o'clock at night, they'd bring in the sprats, empty them all from the river, from the boat, and we used to be in a little shed around a big table, and pick out the sprats, the small sprats was in one tin, and the bigger sprats was in a bigger tin, and then they were sold to the shops. The little ones we used to call them 'muck.' They'd say, 'Oh, they're for sale, and they're for the muck.' I'll tell you who ran it – Mr Worsp. The Worsps was the money people.

The water from out the fish, when they brought them off of the boat, you'd never believe! That was so wet on the floors, you were soaking. I used to stand in this water, with my shoes on, soaked, because my mother couldn't afford boots for us. You smelt terrible! My mother wouldn't have me in the house! My mother used to make me go across over to where the toilet was. She said, 'You ain't coming in here!'

Ivy Knappett

A gallon of shrimps

When I started, they came to the school and wanted the young girls so there was five or six of us went, and some boys. Mr Worsp had his own boats and they were built in Lowestoft. One was *Christine* and one was the *Maid of Wivenhoe*. We picked out the shrimps. Then after a while they got big orders and people took them home to do – a gallon of shrimps.

The shrimps were potted. They were done in those little porcelain white ones. We used to do them with butter – lovely butter – and season, and then put them in these little jars, make a seal, and

Lorry and fish baskets, 1947. (Glendower Jackson)

Above: *Load of sprats, c. 1950. (John Stewart)*

Right: *North Sea Canners, 1947.*
(Glendower Jackson)

they were sent down to the George Hotel and the Red Lion. But I said to Mr Worsp one day, 'We don't have the little pots back.' He said, 'No, they use them for poached egg in the hotels.'

Annie Skilton

Poor chickens

Summer seasons we used to do chickens, when the fish was done. We went on fruit in the autumn. All sorts of fruits. You could bring some yourself and tin them! They used to charge you so much if you tinned them. There was a big yard and we used to have the pens there with the chickens in. Mr Hall was the man who bought the chickens in fresh, daily, all these little spring chickens. Poor little things! I didn't want them to be killed, because they were little spring chickens, you see, and they were put in tins – they were just the right size.

Annie Skilton

The money was good

The money was good then, better money than there was anywhere else, because you were perhaps working till 12 at night, all according to the tide. If the tide was three in the morning, you had to be there at three in the morning.

Ivy Knappett

I could earn more on the bonus than I did on the actual weekly wage. Sometimes I'd do the salmon in tins, sometimes the sardines. You had to grade them by size, fit them in these grooves then put a rod through their eyes and then hang them up on a frame. Big ones, medium ones, small ones, and then they'd go into the big ovens and they'd be grilled, and then the ladies put them in the tins. I've done that as well, putting the fish in tins. We'd shut it down with a vacuum seal. I should think quite a hundred ladies worked there. But I was quite nimble, I could pick up more bonus than I did wages. My wages were £4 and I used to knock a £4 bonus up, £8 was quite a lot of money in 1958. It was smelly, but it was interesting!

Sylvia Weatherall

Imported workers

When I first started, the workers were all local. Then when we got so busy, we had some from Ireland – three or four girls – and a lot of them, they paired off with Wivenhoe boys and married! Lovely girls, we got on all right with them. And then when we were doing sprats we had some girls from Harwich. They had to be brought in by lorry. They were more older people, but they were rough people! At dinner times they used to like going into a pub! And they used to come back and they'd had enough to drink. They didn't stay too long.

Annie Skilton

Alma Street Clothing Factory

A dreadful place

The Alma Street clothing factory was a dreadful place. It was two floors and machines in both floors. Awful toilets. And there were two little anthracite stoves – down the end of the room we were frozen. Absolutely frozen! And you're sitting all the time – only on a little round stool, there was no chairs. And when I first went there to work you weren't given a break, you ate it on the bench, but the law came in – but all we got was this place downstairs in front of the two toilets, to have our break. The smell rises, doesn't it! Awful!

I did all the pockets, and there was another lot of girls seamed the coats up, and then it was passed on to the finishers who finished it all. It was the time of my life, but it was soul-destroying work. Oh, it was dreadful!

Marjorie Goldstraw

Piecework

You got paid according to the quality of the coat. There was silk alpaca, I always remember, and it was dreadful to work on, because it wouldn't press, it shot back each time, and the learners did the back of the coat and the sleeves, and that was about 1/6d a dozen backs and sleeves. When I got on piecework, I did ever so well, and I was taking more than my father. I don't know whether we were well-off, but I could go into Marks and Spencer on a Saturday and get a summer dress. And I always bought the best shoes – Barratts, 'Walk the Barratt way.'

Marjorie Goldstraw

Wivenhoe Sand and Gravel

William G. Loveless opened his gravel pit in 1920 on the eastern fringe of Wivenhoe, soon extending well into Elmstead. The firm stayed in the family until 1961. Becoming a leading figure in the village, Loveless, who enjoyed farming, ran his business with a touch of the country squire.

Mr Loveless had been dabbling in a sand and gravel excavation over at Frating and that ran out, and when he came to live in this area, he got introduced to Frank Pertwee, who said to him, 'How would you like to come to Wivenhoe and open up a gravel pit on that piece of land I've got there?' And [in 1920] he did. But the company was formed in 1925, and that consisted of three directors, i.e. Mr Frank Pertwee and Edgar Lilley, who was the owner a clothing factory in Colchester, and, of course, W.G. Loveless was the third one – he was managing director.

They quarried about twenty-five feet. Beautiful. It was a very very good gravel seam, and on the original fields the topsoil was only about eighteen inches, and then underneath that was some 'hogging,' which was a very red gravel people used for their drives, water it in, and then roll it in tight. And then underneath that there was a little bit of a clay seam, and then beautiful gravel right down to the London Clay, which was about twenty-five feet deep, and that maintained practically right the way across the whole area. It really was a beautiful gravel seam.

Walter Wix

Selling the company

To be honest, [W.G.'s son] Bill Loveless deciding to go into the Church was the reason that they sold the company because of course his father would have much preferred for him to have carried on running the company as a private company. But on the other hand I think there was a problem, inasmuch as the company plant needed reinvestment and the other two directors were not over-keen to commit themselves to putting more money into buying a lot of new plant which, of course, was very necessary and going to be very expensive.

Walter Wix

In the office

Initially [in 1937] clerical-wise there was only [two of us]. And then W.G., the governor himself. He used to do his own thing, write his letters. And then after Bill came, he introduced a lady into the office to help out with the additional work that some of the improvements in the plant created. I didn't take over running the office until '50.

Walter Wix

The pit workforce

There was two separate men who ran the two washing plants. Then we had two loading shovels – a driver for each of those. Then there was somebody who drove the lorry that looked after the bins, and as the bins filled up with the various grades of stone and took them to stockpiles. And then, of course, there was the excavator driver, who was responsible for winning the material from the face. Then there was two dump trucks that used to cart the material down from the face of the pit to the plant. The lorry fleet was gradually increased until we were operating up to twenty vehicles. So there was quite a bit of activity. And then there was the tarmac plant, because another one of Mr Loveless's personal innovations was the introduction of a plant to make tarmacadam, which was pioneering in this particular locality. The stuff they used to call 'Essex mac,' it was his own brand name.

Walter Wix

W.G. Loveless and his men

W.G. Loveless was a good employer. He was a local councillor, he was chairman of the council umpteen times. He was a pillar of the church and a churchwarden and had a lot of interest in the place. I had a lot of respect for him. He looked after his personnel but what he expected from you was loyalty, and a good day's work for a good day's pay.

Even before the War they used to go on an outing every year, [such as to a football match or the theatre]. We were all given pocket money to go to spend. Another feature of Mr Loveless's generosity was at Christmas. Now he used to set a lot of store by Christmas. The land that was not being used for gravel extraction, we used to farm.

And while Mr Loveless was responsible for farming, we used to keep bullocks and pigs and chickens, and he always made sure that everybody had a Christmas dinner. Before the War brought rations, he allocated one of the bullocks, one of the butchers would provide beautiful joints, so that every man had a beef joint for Christmas. And then when there were restrictions, everybody had a turkey or a chicken. He also used to provide a draw of toys and chocolates for the family. And always a great do just before we broke up for Christmas, with all these chickens or the joints and that sort of thing, all laid out with their names on, and then we'd have the draw for the presents, chocolates, or the toys.

Walter Wix

Shops

One of the changes in Wivenhoe life most regretted is the sharp decline in the number of shops, especially in the High Street, where there were twenty shops active in the 1930s, providing for all regular needs. However, then as now, there were also shops at the Cross and scattered elsewhere.

A choice of shops

My mother used to say, 'I don't know what's happened to all our lovely shops we used to have.' Because we used to go down shopping every Thursday and my mum got her pension at the Post Office and my younger sister and me, we all went down shopping, we went down and pay our papers and there were shops you could go to, the butchers, the bakers, and all that – you can't do that sort of thing now. I think it's a shame.

Ellen Primm

We had everything

We had three butchers – Mr Rivens, Mr Everett, Mr King. Three bakers – Miss Franks, Mr Last, Mr Cracknell. And two lovely grocers shops –Jimmy Moore and Stacey Woods, beautiful grocers. You'd go in and you could smell the coffee. That was always weighed. And then we had a household shop where you could buy curtains, towels, sheets, anything in that line. A chemist – Mr Corlip. Newsagents. Three sweet shops – Mrs Blutts, Mrs Barrett, Mrs Stewart. And of course Mr Green, the fish shop. And there was a cycle shop. Mrs Bailey sold clothes, shoes, anything to wear. And Mr Chaney, hardware, all nails and hammers and paraffin oil. Really you didn't need to go out of Wivenhoe in those days. Now there's nothing.

Edna Wadley

Shops on the Cross

We used the shops on the Cross, as a kid, the Post Office there, and a little shop beside it, where they sold anything from cottons to elastics, and notebooks, and sweets. I used to shop at the Co-Op for Mother, and for the week's shopping, she used to give me ten bob and you got change out of it! I think the demise of the shops in Wivenhoe, it's sad to think that you had two bakers, three butchers shops, and about six general stores, at least – that's

besides the Co-op. When you think that all those people relied on a business of about 2,100 people in the village, and now we've got 10,000.

Ray Hall

Highly prized ironmonger

There were various shopkeepers which were important, they were somebody in the village. They definitely had a status. The most highly prized man was Percy Chaney and everybody used to call him 'Uncle Percy.' He had the ironmonger's shop opposite the old Post Office, and a paraffin store round the back – of course, lots of the lighting was paraffin oil lights. And he had this kind of shop which had been stocked in about 1900 and never replenished! And I went there in 1954 and I wanted a pair of two-way hinges. You couldn't buy them anywhere. I went and saw Mr Chaney and he said, 'I've got some upstairs somewhere.' He had a loft to that place and he went out and about twenty minutes later he came down with two pairs of magnificent brass hinges that had been ordered for a yacht in about 1920 and he'd still got them in

Barrell's newsagent and tobacconist, 1963. (Jan Frostick))

High Street with one of the Moore twins outside their shop, 1900s. (Don Smith)

the loft! He had a telephone in the shop. So if you needed a telephone – not that we knew anybody with a telephone – Uncle Percy Chaney would use it for you. You didn't go round the counter. But I can't imagine anybody in Wivenhoe wanting to use the telephone, to be quite honest.

Dennis Sparling

Fabulous grocers

There were two main grocery shops, other than the little ones in people's front rooms. One was Stacey Woods. The other was the brothers Moore – who were marvellous old boys. It was part of that Grosvenor complex. And it was an absolutely fabulous shop. They used to wear black waistcoats and white aprons down to their ankles and they always looked exactly the same. They had those marvellous little drawers with all the spices, all done in mahogany, beautifully made. And mirrors. And the lovely marble counter at the far end with the bacon slicer on, and you went and asked for bacon and they'd cut it off. And just inside the door there was a huge – for a small child – terrifying big trap door, and that's where they kept the wine. I can remember a big 'patent medicines' jar on the counter. They sold absolutely everything. You had these little blue bags and they'd measure out the tea or sugar. They had lovely pairs of scales, with all the brass – everything polished. It was all completely different. And all biodegradable of course!

Halcyon Palmer

The baker's oven

Miss Franks had a bakery in East Street, and I used to deliver bread on Saturdays for her up at the Cross/Rectory Road area. The bicycle had a little wheel on the front and a huge basket, and when that was loaded with bread it was as much as I could do to pedal it. Often I used to fall over, and the bread would go all over the road! People would say, 'The bread's dirty.' I'd say, 'Well, that's how it came out of the oven'!

Glendower Jackson

Next door was the bakery where people took their dinners, because those ovens stopped hot, and every day people took their dinner there. Just stick it in the oven and it'd cook it, although the oven had gone off.

Marjorie Goldstraw

Fish and chips

Harry Chambers, the High Street, he was a cobbler. Take my shoes off, have them soled and heeled, call at the fish shop, get fish and chips to take home for the dinner on Saturday. I used to have enough change left out of that, after getting my shoes soled and heeled, for fish and chips for the whole family, with a big bag of crackle that come off the batter for about a penny. Oh, that used to be lovely!

Charles Tayler

Mr Sainty's ice cream

Mr Sainty had a shop, a wooden little hut on the left-hand side, a little before the turning to Manor Road, and he sold biscuits and groceries and sweets and the most wonderful icecream! You've never tasted icecream like Mr Sainty made! He made it himself. It was custardy – oh, it was lovely! In the back room of the shop he'd got the machinery to make it, it crushed up the ice and it used to make a noise and you said 'Oh, he's making icecream!'

Olive Whaley

Bottling the milk

In Belle Vue Road there was Reg Beckwith's little sweetshop and milk shop. Well, I lived next door but one. And my brother used to go to Lennox Farm up the Cross, and milk the cows and bring the milk down in a churn. At the back of the shop, in the garden, he had a little dairy, Mr Beckwith, and I used to go in there every day and bottle the milk. I think I drank half of it, actually! Pour the milk in the top and it ran down like, a radiator with cooling water in it, into an urn at the bottom and I would do the bottling – pint, and half pint, and two pint bottles. And they had a waxed disc top on them.

Glendower Jackson

Hygiene standards

There was a shop in Queen's Road which was the funniest shop out! I mean, hygiene standards weren't observed at all in those days! You'd find sacks of sugar with little mice creeping about round them and nibbling holes in the bottom and that sort of thing! But it didn't seem to affect us!

Joyce Blackwood

Drapery shop assistant

For my first job when I left school I went into Mrs Lily Parker's drapery shop. My mother had always known Mrs Parker and unbeknown to me had said to her if Doris, this other girl, is leaving any time, 'I'd like my daughter to come and work with you.' 'Oh,' said Mrs Parker, 'I'd like it.' And as soon as she knew this other girl was leaving she saw my mother and said could I start? And I got on ever so well with her. It was quite a biggish shop. It sold clothes, socks, children's socks, knickers and underwear, and wool, and materials, almost everything, because people didn't go in to Colchester to shop very much in those days. If anybody wanted anything special Mrs Parker would get it for them.

Freda Annis

Pension club

It was like a club out there [the Post Office], particularly on Mondays or Thursdays, in the old days. All the pensions were paid on a Thursday but in the latter years anybody new coming on to a pension was paid on a Monday. So you had almost two clubs – the more elderly were on a Thursday and the younger pensioners were on a Monday. And they were like a Thursday club and a Monday club! They'd been chatting outside, came in to do their bits, get their pension, pay the bills and buy savings stamps – in those days you could buy stamps towards your telephone bill, your gas bill, electricity bill, TV licence, all sorts of things. So this is how a lot of them budgeted because none of them had bank accounts, they just had the cash and allocated it for the various bits and pieces.

David Burrows

Opening Wivenhoe Bookshop in 1975: Jean Harding and Penny Bell. (Jean Harding)

The 'pub ladies' hair

I used to do what I called all the 'pub ladies' hair. There was Mrs Cabuche from the Black Buoy, there was the lady from the Station Hotel, there was the lady from the Horse & Groom, and the Brewery, that was the sister-in-law of the lady that worked in the Black Buoy. The Rose & Crown – Mrs Sparrow. So I just used to go around and just have a drink with them, just to feel that they were kind enough to give me their business – not that they'd make a lot out of me! But we all knew each other, that was the point. And now I don't think people do so much, in the village.

Jan Frostick

Wivenhoe bookshop

One was very surprised that no one had done it [opened a bookshop] before. Quite honestly, I wouldn't actually have wanted it if the University hadn't been there. That was a very important part of it. It came to be much more so than we had realised, later on. They were wonderful in giving us quite large orders right from the beginning.

We had three launch parties [in 1976], all in three days. My husband at that time was still with the BBC, directing on the *Book Programme*, fortunately! So we went rather high up for the first launch because he was working with Christina Foyle, who

was the owner of the Foyle's Bookshop, which boasted itself as being the largest bookshop in the world. So Christina Foyle very kindly came over to open what we described as 'probably the smallest bookshop in the world'!

In March 1977 we had a local authors' week. We had Michael Frost, John Leather, and Alan Watts, all of whom were sailing people. John Leather used to come in very regularly and check the shelves to make sure we'd got a full complement of all his books! We had a very good stock of maritime material. A mixture of sailing and flying, actually. And there was Jessie Hickford and her guide dog – she was local. We had Margery Dean, and Elizabeth Jeffrey, and Jack Cross, and Leila Berg and Susannah Bradley, these are all our local authors.

Penny Bell and Jean Harding

Door to Door

When we moved here in 1963 we had a lot of people who used to call twice a week with a van or a lorry, so on Tuesday and Friday there would be greengrocery, and on Wednesday it would be the butcher, there was a lot of that. It was terrific service. You don't realise it until you haven't got it any more.

Halcyon Palmer

The milkman Mr Beckwith came with his milk in a big urn thing, and he'd got his measure and mum would bring the jug to the door and he'd measure it out and she'd say, 'I want to make a rice pudding today, Reg.' So she'd bring the dish for the rice pudding and put it straight in!

Olive Whaley

My mother, being a Rowhedge person, used to still get her meat from Rowhedge, and a chap used to come over with his basket on the front and several people in Wivenhoe used to have him, although there was at least two butchers' shops in Wivenhoe at the time. He come over on the ferry, come up through the Toll Gate, tuppence a bike!

Ray Hall

Delivery boy

When I was fourteen I used to be quite an industrious lad! I used to be a paperboy in the mornings, during the week – Monday to Saturday. A paperboy on a Sunday for a different person – the Shipwrights' Arms, and then eventually to Hall's in Queen's Road. Then I was Jimmy Moore's grocery boy – on a bike. And that was an hour every afternoon except Thursdays, plus Saturday mornings. Who did I deliver to? I hate to say the word 'class,' but a few of the uppermost paid people, school teachers, the curator of Colchester Castle Museum – he lived in Wivenhoe. Old ship captains and suchlikes.

Alan Green

In Business

TV trade

I've been in the TV trade all my life. I started in it at fifteen years old, served my National Service, and then came out and went back to it again. After I came out of the Army I married Carol, a local girl, and came to Wivenhoe in 1959. I worked for a company in Colchester for eleven years and then decided time was for me to have a go at my own. So I found a shop in Wivenhoe, 29 High Street. Then we took over No. 31 and joined the two to make one large one. I started off as a one-man business in 1969, but after a few months I got so much business I needed somebody to give me help, so I took a partner on, Mr Stevens, another TV engineer. That's where we got the 'Allcock & Stevens' from. In the early days, of course, people were still listening to radios. I started when accumulators were still around. I remember the 'Cat's Whisker,' that was the first one. When we started we were nearly all black and white TVs – there were very few colour sets around. The boom times were a couple of years

ahead of us, and then we were selling an awful lot of colour TVs because once mass production got going our business took off. This ran along right into the early Eighties. We had a rental content, which was very healthy, but as TVs became more reliable rental went into decline quite a bit.

Tony Allcock

Fish and chip shop

My father had a stroke just before we packed up [fishing] and we had the chance to take the shop. He'd worked there as a boy, he knew the fish trade backwards. So we said we'd sell the boat and take the shop. Well, we sold the boat and he died. So I was then left with the option of taking over the shop – which I didn't know much about and didn't know if I wanted to know that much about it, not on my own. But, anyhow, I started the shop going and I thought, 'Well, stay there for six months' just get it up and running and get another boat and go back to sea'. But then the fishing got worse and I was making a living and I was beginning to enjoy what I was doing there. I stayed there for thirty-six years!

Brian Green

Smoking the Yarmouth herring

The Yarmouth herring came already salted, from Lowestoft. But we would do our own bloatering – that's smoking the herring whole. And the smell of everyone cooking those bloaters all over Wivenhoe was superb! Because everyone had their own smoke hole of yesteryear. And that gradually died out, but as we kept our own smoking going, we were the last family which did our own smoking. We smoked our own haddocks without dye added. We smoked our own bloaters in smokehouses built on Bowes's Marshes, and as a kid I used to play in the sawdust. It had to be oak sawdust, not pine, not softwood. Hardwood. Elm was okay. Never pine, otherwise it would be the wrong flavour. Those smokehouses were where the Wivenhoe Sailing Club is now.

Peter Green

Smokehouses

We had a smoking kiln in the new shop that we built in Colchester, and it was called a 'mechanical curing kiln.' The interesting thing was that the prototype was built in Wivenhoe by North Sea Canners, by Lewis Worsp in conjunction with Torry Research. And I use that method today. But I have smoked in the traditional manner as well. In fact I've even burnt two smokehouses down in my time! One was in my brother Douglas's back garden and another one, you'll never believe, was in the middle of the river! We had a concrete barge, which was in Mr Worsp's Dock, and I built a smokehouse out on the end that stuck right out in the middle of the river.

Ken Green

The miller's scales

The Mill House, on the corner of Rectory Road and Belle Vue Road, was still being run as a grain and livestock feed merchant – Mr Mortlock – a little tiny man with little bandy legs. I think his family had been in that business for generations. Their little brown pony and Mousy, from the mill, would deliver the animal feed and grain. They had great big scales to weigh the sacks of grain and animal feed stuff. Behind those two rather ugly houses in Belle Vue Road there was a long, low series of barns which smelled lovely of grain and flour – just a wonderful countryside smell. I used to stand on the scales to keep a check on my health and growth. They were huge.

Sue Kerr

Building craftsmen

I got a job with Masons, a Wivenhoe building firm who were building the council houses, that my father was doing a lot of work for. The firm took me on as a labourer and I learnt my trade with them. Masons were at the end of Belle Vue Road, near where the old mill was. The boss, Walter Mason, ran the building business. And Percy Blanche was the other carpenter. They were quite characters, typical country craftsmen who had been in the trade all their lives, and probably their fathers before them. Walter was a canny old craftsman. He made some wonderful oak settles, like they used to have in the old pubs, with the carved beads on the ends. He used to spend all his spare time after work in the workshop, making these settles and little coal boxes out of oak.

Gilbert Whaley

Throw away the old saw

We had so much more time to do a job! Comparatively, wages were so much lower than what the materials were – the materials were the expensive part of the job, and the labour was cheap, whereas now, it's the other way round. We just waste and throw away, it makes you sad but it's not worth picking it up and

William Sparrow & Son, builders, 1985, with William Sparrow junior. (Dennis Marsden)

salvaging it and storing it. But labour – you can't let anybody sit still for a minute. So it's completely the opposite to how it was.

If it was raining, we'd paint scaffold tubes, or just do odd jobs in the yard, and now, there's nothing to do in the yard like that. You'd have to send people home and not pay them, you can't afford to say, 'Well, you know, the weather's a bit inclement, we'll stay in and we'll sort out the workshop.'

None of the maintenance jobs get done, basically. I'm sure it applies throughout. People don't get time to do things. Everything we throw away – we don't sharpen saw blades, we just throw them away and buy a new one, because I can't pay a carpenter to set and sharpen his saw, because he can spend an hour doing that, and [for the cost of an hour's wages] I can buy a brand new saw, which will be sharper than he'll ever get his one that he'll sharpen. So I just bring a new one back and he throws the old one away.

William Sparrow

Coal business

I had two uncles and they ran the local coal business, and they lived in the arch in the High Street. The coal used to come in on the train, where they call the engine shed now, and they used to store it on the marshes.

Betty Govan

Impecunious but aesthetic

My mother was a historian. After the War she opened a mail order antique business from our home, which subsequently grew and she had a gallery. But it started just after the War when you had to have coupons to buy furniture, and it was very difficult for young married people to buy furniture for their houses and so she put an advertisement in the *New Statesman* saying, 'Impecunious but aesthetic? Send for catalogue, to Margery Dean,' and she built up a very good business doing that. We had all sorts of interesting people who used to come.

Halcyon Palmer

Starting at Wivenhoe Cross Post Office

We started on 31 January, '86. The Post Office – we always ended on a Friday in those days, so we started on a Saturday morning. We had some training, we had a trainer with us for a week, but the training was hit and miss, so we were fortunate in having two brothers with Post Offices, I could always get on the phone and say, 'How do you do this?' So, it was in at the deep end.

Friday night was always a traumatic night for the first few weeks, because you had to balance the books on a Friday night, ready for the next week. We were taught the official way, which means you didn't start anything until after the office had shut. At half past five, you started to count everything down to the last penny stamp, to make sure that everything tallied and what have you! So I suppose it was about 10 o'clock by the time we finished!

David Burrows

Just winding me up

The first Thursday, I can always remember, and it was something I hadn't sort of quite bargained for, the pure number of people who came for pensions on a Thursday morning! There was just an enormous queue that built up, obviously we were much slower at dealing with everything, in those days, because we were so new to it. And one of the funny things – funny now, I didn't think so at the time – but this great big voice at the back of the queue said, 'New postmaster's taking his time! Does he think we've got all day?' I didn't know how to take it to start with, he was just winding me up, which was fine! But in later years, I could reciprocate and wind him up, just as easily!

David Burrows

Welcome cake

One of the nice things, on the very first day that we opened on the Saturday morning, I suppose it was about 11 o'clock, a little old lady came in, Aileen Style – she used to live in the Ropery House just along here – came in with her tin of cakes, and just said, 'Welcome to the Cross,' which was really nice! And that made us very very welcome. That was quite nice really, because in later years, when she was on her own, we could reciprocate, by taking her a Christmas dinner when we dished them out, we just used to take one along to her. We were two strangers – we were just made so welcome.

David Burrows

Facing Challenges

Chandlers

My father had a ships' chandlers shop, and he was on a damn good thing when he was young and all the yachts were about. But it fell through after the First World War and he sold the shop and he worked in an office in a sand works at Fingringhoe after that. The shop was a corner shop, with steps right on the corner and Mr Bowes's cows used to make a mess on there every time they went round! It was a small shop – double-decker, you'd got a store room up top. Used to sell paraffin and paints, ships' paints and screws and – well, everything. My grandfather was a skipper on a big steam yacht and so of course all the yachts used to get the paint from dad's, to please grandfather I suppose! And they were Masons, I think!

Pat Ellis

Sail-maker

Hector Barr was sail-maker in what is now the Nottage, and I remember one of his orders was for 80,000 kit bags! That's a piece of an order! He must have nearly fell over – but this was wartime and that was for the Navy. Most of the men had gone off to the War and so he employed the ladies locally. I think that's why he packed up, yachting had diminished a lot and there was no people sailing yachts at the end of the War. So he packed up, but I think he was sorry for it afterwards.

Jimmy Lawrence

Business rivalry

There was another hairdressers, Cyril Brown's on the corner of West Street. I think Cyril Brown took it quite hard that I started near him. I used to have an extractor fan in the window because I'd got no opening windows and no back, and he'd walk past and I'd hear him saying, 'Flash in the pan. Flash in the pan.' Well, I only lasted for two and a half years but I sold it as a going concern.

Jan Frostick

Tremendous support

I never wanted the business to get big – we were always going to be happy with a small business. Sell yourself first, the product second, and you'll get there. I think you can be the hard businessman but it doesn't always work for you if you are, because you're going to be a very lonely person at some time or other. With Waites, the other TV shop in Wivenhoe, we've always worked side by side – they've always been more on the electrical side, and we've always got on well together. We're here to help you if we can, and advice comes free. If you can be friendly to everybody – and it doesn't take a lot of energy – you generally find the public respond to you. Early on in the business we did have tremendous support from Wivenhoe, from local people. Without them, we would never have existed.

But as time goes along people change and more new people move into the area. Well, yes, it gives us extra work, but nowhere near as much as anybody would think because most of the people bring their own TVs with them. But if someone moves in and they call you round to connect their TV up, we go and do that. I like to think that you gives a good first impression. And with our trade there's always been advancing. When videos were introduced we moved on into them and hi-fi equipment, and CDs – compact discs – came in, taking over from the records and the tapes. Everything was advancing very very fast – and still is.

Tony Allcock

Egg lifter

One of our old pensioners used to toddle along to the butchers for his weekend joint. Now, the butcher always had trays of eggs on the customers' side of the counter and this pensioner, he used to slip a couple of eggs into his pocket, unbeknown to the butcher. Till all of a sudden the butcher latched on and once he had, he sauntered out from his side of the counter and he accidentally nudged this particular customer in the pocket! And needless to say the eggs stopped disappearing after that!

David Burrows

A new estate agent

A little shop came up in Wivenhoe and I decided to go for it, and then hit the worst recession that the housing industry had ever had for seven years! So that was an absolute nightmare for several years. I opened in February '88. It was freezing cold. There was no heating in the shop. I'd got one really crappy old desk a friend had given me with a twizzle chair that I fell off every time I turned round! The phone wouldn't reach the desk and I daren't move the desk to where the phone was because I thought people won't see I'm there. And I had the door open all the time so that people would come in but nobody did. I was sitting there in my sheepskin jacket and gloves and woollies because I'd never been so cold. But after a couple of weeks I got four houses – they were friends of mine!

Ann Quarrie

Struggling and closing

The last five years of our trading we were struggling. Supermarkets being allowed to open on Sundays was one of the nails in the coffin. Trade dropped a lot. And then the last nail in the coffin was when Tesco opened at Hythe. After that our trade went down. And when we actually retired we never had no capital by us but the shop belonged to us. We tried to sell the business for five years and in that five years we only had about ten people come and have a look. And the people who came

and had a look were husband and wife and they said they'd never been in the greengrocery business before and he used to think, 'Oh, that's simple, just buying and selling,' and the wife would run the business and the husband would go out to work. It weren't till we show them around and told them about what the potatoes was and what they had to do, they realised that it is a two-man job, it's a husband and wife – it's a partnership. We couldn't sell it as a business and we just said, 'Right, we'll put it up as a house,' and that went the next day to a cash buyer!

Pat Green

Pubs

There were over twenty pubs in Wivenhoe in 1900, including four going back at least to the eighteenth century, compared with only six today. But the pubs are still a crucial part of the flavour of Wivenhoe's social life. Included below are memories from Dennis Sparling and Glendower Jackson who grew up in the Station and the Grosvenor in the 1930s, and Colin Andrews who ran the Station in the 1980s.

A Choice of Pubs

There were twenty-three pubs when my mum was a girl! Twenty-three, just imagine! And the only time my dad went to the pub was when he had his union meetings at the Park Hotel and my mother used to give him tuppence for half a pint of beer after he had his meeting! And that used to tickle me! I said, 'You're just allowed a half, then, Dad?' He said, 'Yes, I'm not allowed any more!'

Ellen Primm

The Trade Union Club Room

At the Station Hotel there was a 'club room' and it held about 30 people. The Railway Union used to meet there, the Boilermakers' Union. I can remember it because each society had a really big tin chest with their names on and two locks, so as the secretary and somebody had to be there before you could undo the locks. But also it was our playroom, it was part of our house. The only thing was, the kitchen was three floors below!

Dennis Sparling

Apprentice boys

So we used to come to Wivenhoe, all the apprentice boys came to Wivenhoe, and we used to go to the Station Hotel about eight o'clock, pay your union, you'd have a small brown there, and then we would go out round the pubs of Wivenhoe. Usually used to walk along West Street, towards the Shipwrights' Arms, and have a look in there, if there was too many people in there, there weren't enough glasses to have a drink, so we used to go along from there sometimes down on to the Quay, but more than likely head for the Black Buoy, which was a much more lively pub, and then either to the Brewer's round near the Yard, or to the Falcon Hotel, and gradually work our way up the street, having one or two, and a good Friday night was had by all the apprentices!

John Bines

Drinks for commuters

In those days, people used to travel from Brightlingsea to London, on a daily basis, commuting in. And what used to happen was that they used to come from Liverpool Street into Wivenhoe, on a direct line, and they used to get off at Wivenhoe, and the Brightlingsea line train was in the sidings. So once the Clacton line had gone through – this puffer came through – the Brightlingsea 'Crab and Winkle' and picked the people up, on the station, who lived in Brightlingsea. But, of course, in that time, which took something like seven or eight minutes, they all used to rush across the bridge, and we had all the drinks lined up, and they used to come in and have all their drinks, and then go back and catch the train!

This happened every night of the working week. And they would all settle their bills at the end of the week. They were clerks in banks and things, and

they wore suits! They didn't go to work in overalls like the rest of the men in the village .

Dennis Sparling

No women

[In the 1940s] women didn't go to pubs! I can remember we lived next door to a pub, the Falcon, and on a Saturday night they sometimes danced on the tables and I can remember my mother just being horrified! We thought it was terribly exciting!

Halcyon Palmer

Granny had got a sense of humour. She used to like to tell us all these tales! But the Greyhound has got their room, you go up the steps to it. Well, of course they weren't allowed to go in the pub, but apparently there were several of them got with a few boys and they used to go there and they used to have a sly drink. And one night somebody went in and he said, 'You want to watch it!' There was my granny and her sister – Hannah and Edith. He said, 'Your father's coming up the road.' So they couldn't go out the front way, so one of the boys helped them out the back window and they went out of the back of the Greyhound, down Brook Hill [now Queen's Road], they ran all the way down the hill, across the railway line, and when father comes back they're sitting indoors!

Freda Annis

Beer for maiden ladies

Saturdays was spent pushing a barrow round the village delivering all beer orders mainly to people who didn't drink in the pub. Bottles of beer to maiden ladies who didn't appear to drink! One or two who had quite a lot more than anybody would ever suspect! I had a barrow and I did it from the time I was eleven or twelve.

Dennis Sparling

Floor scrubbing

My mother used to work in the Black Buoy on the Quay. And she used to take me up to the Black Buoy after nine at night and she scrubbed the floor – there was no lino, there was just wood, like – and she used to scrub that and scrub that after all the beer was soaked in where they'd dropped it. Now, I went down there not so very long ago because I had a girl staying here from abroad and oh, the difference it was! All nice tablecloths on the table – and when I used to go in there, old wood floor!

Ivy Knappett

Station sanitation

[At the Station Hotel] originally the sewage was put on in 1931, and the house itself had proper flush toilets in when we moved in 1935, but the public rooms had what was called a 'bumby,' which was a toilet facility over a big garden shed. Like an earth closet. But it was dug out every week or so. A very unsavoury business – the night soil cart used to come round and collect all the sewage.

Dennis Sparling

Hearse & Gloom

The Horse & Groom was run by Harry and his wife, who got the nickname for the pub, the 'Hearse & Gloom,' because he didn't tolerate people having too good a time. He would only sell people one packet of cigarettes at a time, things like that.

Pat Smith

Sick of the sight

My grandfather was not, perhaps, the most popular man in some ways! He was a landlord [of the Rose & Crown], he liked that bit, he didn't really like any of his customers, he just got sick of them. I can always remember them saying, that people would wait outside the door for you to open, and it was the same faces that you'd seen the day before, and you had to put on a smile for them, because they'd be your best customers, but you're really sick of the sight of them! They're there from 6.30 till 11.30, apart from Sundays every day of the week, and he used to stand there behind the bar, listening to a lot of beer talk, a lot of rubbish.

William Sparrow

Smuggling and the last days of the Falcon

The Falcon Inn must go back almost as far as the church. It was both a pub and a hotel and for many years the most successful hostelry in Wivenhoe. It was where all the election meetings were held, all the auctions were held, where the yacht owners would come when they were looking after their yachts. Elizabeth Jeffrey has written a nice book, *Cassie Jordan*, which is essentially a novel about the house. When I first knew the building it was in a very run-down condition. The hotel was pretty moribund. The Park Hotel had taken over from it and the pub was run by a strange Pole called Stefan. He had been a member of the Polish Free Forces during the War and told improbable stories about his exploits in Italy. The Falcon was decorated with some of his war memorabilia. He kept a not very good pub. But he had the great advantage of speaking Polish and when the Port developed a timber importing trade, whereby ships came twice a week from Gdansk laden with timber to Wivenhoe, Stefan began a very active vodka smuggling business. Stacks of timber were hollowed out and vodka was put there. The odd case here or there didn't matter, but when it got to trailer load of quantities the revenue decided this was beyond a joke! Staked out the top of the church and caught him red-handed. So Stefan went to jail and [in the early 1970s] the brewery decided to put the property on the market.

John Ashworth

The Station or the Rose & Crown

Simon Smith had the Station in the late Eighties/ Nineties. The Port was open then too, and that changed its character. The Station was regarded as quite a rough place because of the docks and dockworkers and the crews from the coasters – the ships that used to come into the Port here, maybe stay overnight. I always found it quite friendly.

The Station was a more masculine type of pub than, say, the Rose & Crown, where you get people who want to sit and look at the river. Mind you, at the Station you could sit and look at the ships.

Vic Pillkington, at the Rose & Crown, he was a great character. Vic was very funny, told stories and he'd dress up in fancy dress. He was a dead ringer! And he used to serve his regulars before the tourists – he made a point of that. 'Regulars first.'

Max Tannahill

Pub Games and Fun

The Horse & Groom then was like a traditional Essex pub with little compartments, and the ladies were in one side of the compartment and the men were the other, and the barmaid was on our side and we'd be putting the world to rights in our little corner every Friday night. And I remember Wally Whymark – a well known local character – he used to shout behind the barrier, 'Did you get that, Ethel?' if any gossip was going on. Before long that gossip was all round the village, of course!

Bill Heslop

Shipwrights in the Grosvenor

It was always the shipwright men that went to the pub. As soon as the whistle blew they were in the pub. They would be there playing darts and all sitting around. They always sang songs. There would always be somebody in there who could play a little piano accordion thing, a little squeezebox. And there were always dart matches – quite often they would ask me to pick the darts up if they threw and hit and they'd bounce off and they'd give me a halfpenny at the end of the evening.

Glendower Jackson

Vic Pilkington, landlord of the Rose & Crown. (Dennis Marsden)

Pub divisions and pub games

The [Station] pub was divided into three bits. There was the bar, which was really the kind of stand up and have a drink type place. Then there was the smoke room which was where you played dominoes and darts. And then there was the parlour, where you only played solo whist while you all sit round. The working-class blokes didn't play solo whist, they played darts and dominoes and cribbage.

Card games were not played in the pub on a Sunday. The dart board was closed, and cards and dominoes, were not played You could play solo whist, and you could play cribbage. But you couldn't play nap, and you couldn't play darts. So in the summertime, when it was a Sunday, other things would happen. And we had a game called 'Tip It.' You had two long tables with people, and they all sat side by side, perhaps eight or ten aside, with their hands under the table, and then you'd

Railway footbridge and Station Hotel. (Don Smith)

We used to have one man who came in [to the Station] every Saturday night and he played the piano for drinks. Bill Snelling. And his son used to come, when he was about thirteen, and played the violin and he was an absolutely fine violinist – both of them untutored or self-taught as far as I know. Mr Snelling worked at Paxmans Diesels. Lots of things that went on in a village pub wouldn't be countenanced in the towns! When you got somebody who could play the piano the whole pub sang – it was more the maudlin type songs, in the main. They used to sing 'Come into the Garden, Maud.'

Dennis Sparling

pass a coin up and down the table, and you'd bring your hands up, and somebody on the other side had to guess which hand held the coin.

Dennis Sparling

In the old days you'd go in the Rose & Crown, there'd be six old boys playing dominoes and the first thing, they wanted us to play with them – only to get a free pint – but it was fun! We used to go in there and they'd say, 'Want to have a game of dominoes, boy?'

Peter Sainty

At the Station Hotel we had a quoits rink. It was at the back of the pub – that space was all open ground when I was a child which was a bed of clay, and the whole object was to be able to throw this 8lb steel disk and get it nearest to the pin.

Dennis Sparling

Pub music

In the forties when Alf Gooch kept the Flag, Ken Hodges played the piano and a Univox organ on the end of it. My husband played drums. Ken Hodges played so he could pay for his first television. My husband played for the children's dinner money. They used to play Saturday night and Sunday night, for a pound. All they got was a pound.

Eunice Baker

An exercise in sociology

Running the Station Hotel was a good exercise in sociology! I'd recommend it to anybody in sociology! You get all the characters in there – truly cosmopolitan. You could have academics but you could also have road sweepers or whatever, they all joined together in there and it was quite a levelling process. Because the early evening customers were businessmen dropping in for an early drink who wanted to be entertained, that was joke time. Sometimes I used to write a script, and have a prompt card under the counter, just to run off a few jokes and keep everything going!

Colin Andrews

Caring for drinkers

It was mainly the problem of a very few people, there were one or two who were known heavy drinkers, and they were never a problem. Although they got drunk, because you lived with them, they lived with you, you knew them. It was much more, 'Oh, who's going to see Fred home tonight?' Or, 'If you're going up, take him with you.'

Dennis Sparling

five

Professions, Services and the Churches

The `Crab and Winkle' for Brightlingsea at Wivenhoe station, 1953. (John Stewart)

In the 1940s, when the National Health Service was launched, free medical care was a novelty, but also there were far fewer known effective treatments for illness.

The railways were still the most important form of transport, but Cedric's Garage had opened in 1928. The children in the village school in Phillip Road were securely under the thumb of their head teacher, Miss Smith, and the churches were a crucial part of everyday life in the village.

Doctors

Lord God Almighty!

When you were ill you didn't send for a doctor. And on rare occasions when my mother had to, she spring-cleaned the whole house because the doctor in those days was Lord God Almighty!

It's all changed! For infectious diseases you could have a vaccination, but my mother wouldn't have us done. But there wasn't anything else. I had fits when I had measles. You were really ill. Terrible. Hospital was the last resort! You nursed people at home and they used to spread straw in the road, for the noise.

Marjorie Goldstraw

Kitchen table operation

I do remember, clearly, having my tonsils out on the kitchen table in the Grosvenor Hotel. And the operation was done by a man called Dr Evans, who had his house in East Bay in Colchester. And he came down to the pub in a horse and trap and he did the operation on the kitchen table, and my father held the bucket while he snipped, snipped, and he took my adenoids out at the same time! And he charged my father two bottles of whisky! And before he left he'd drunk half of one of the bottles! And he was so drunk that my father had to take his pony and trap and point it up the High Street, put Dr Evans in the seat, and give him the reins, and he slapped the horse and it went trotting away up the High Street, back to Colchester, East Bay, on its own!

Glendower Jackson

Appendix operation

There was a man, he was the first one in the Colchester Hospital to have appendix out and he died. And I was the second one in Colchester Hospital, a child. I was about the first one in Wivenhoe who had appendix. When I went to Yarmouth on the train from Wivenhoe I sat with the train driver, and they took me there for convalescence and I was there for three weeks. You see, I was only about ten or eleven in those days. I think I went for nothing. Nobody had money those days. And then they sent me home but they wouldn't allow me to take my shoes off or my socks off in case I broke the stitches. But now look at them, they go in the morning to have appendix out and they're playing around after tea!

Ivy Knappett

Whooping cough

In 1931 there was a whooping cough epidemic and I was actually born with whooping cough. Quite a few children died of whooping cough and so did their mothers. And the perceived wisdom in those days was that whooping cough could be cured or alleviated by going down the gasworks, in Gas Road, down past the old Fire Station. And, of course you had huge sulphurous emissions so it was deemed that this was good for children with whooping cough.

Dennis Sparling

Doctors Dean and Radcliffe

Wivenhoe was very partisan. You either went to see Dr William Dean or you went to see Dr Walter Radcliffe, and there were almost pitched battles fought as to who was the best doctor in Wivenhoe!

Dr Dean lived on the corner of Alma Street and his waiting room, dispensary, and the consulting room was in a rather ramshackle single-storey building behind the main house. Of course the doctor was available night and day, on call. He did his own dispensing. He was a very quietly-spoken man, very kind, very gentle and informal. Smoked a pipe. Always looked as if he'd just come in from the garden! Very ramshackle!

Sue Kerr

Margery and William [Dean] were passionate readers of the *New Statesman*, and a very much *avant garde* couple. He was the local doctor, and sweet, rather scatterbrained and eccentric. And so everything about Wivenhoe didn't exactly fit into the normal expectation of an English village! William was our doctor. Wasn't he a bit of a bully, the other one? But maybe the stories told about him came from the Dean camp. William was really, I think, probably more interested in antiques, than he was in medicine.

Sir Peregrine Worsthorne

Dr Walter Radcliffe was slim, very brisk, always in a starched white coat, rather formal. Quite a different man to Dr Dean. He had a French wife, a very pretty lady nicknamed 'Bunny.' And he was also a talented amateur boat designer.

Sue Kerr

You did your best

We weren't threatened with being sued. Most patients, certainly when I arrived here, were quite certain that you would do your best for them and if it didn't work or if something went wrong, well, you did your best. That meant that you could do your best.

Over that time I noticed changes not in the illnesses that they had, as much as their reactions to them. Patients now don't expect to be ill, and they expect immediate cures. A nice little story! I once went to see a patient and I said to him, 'Look, you've got the flu here, you stay in bed until I come again and I'll have another look at you.' And I didn't note it down, I completely forgot him. And I met him in a pub about six months later and he

said, 'Doc, I'm sorry, I just couldn't wait any longer!' This was a failure on my part but the patients took very much that attitude. And they were always very thankful if you came out and saw them at night.

Dr Ted Palmer

Wivenhoe disease

Alcoholism – 'Wivenhoe disease!' Oh yes, serious trouble. So you tell them. So what? I looked after several of them and they knew. I mean, oh God! They knew that they were killing themselves but kill themselves they did. And there's no way you can stop them if they want to do it.

Dr Ted Palmer

Paternalism

We were extremely paternalistic in the attitude that we took. We would never bring in the Social Services if we could avoid it. We tried never ever to bring in the police. The odd bit of incest and all the other minor things, once the Social Services got it, well, it broke up the family and it destroyed everything. I know it's a terrible thing to say but – anyway, because I'm a deconstructed man now! – we would sort it out. With incest I would go and see them and I would see the chap involved and I would say, 'Look here, lad. If it comes to my notice again…'

Dr Ted Palmer

Transport and Services

The Toll Gate

The Toll Gate [on the road to the Rowhedge ferry] had a big five-barred gate with spikes on top – and I can remember the big black board now, telling you what the tariffs were. It was about a penny if you was on foot, threepence for a horse, and the doctor was free. It was quite a high gate, you'd have a job to get over it without paying.

Jimmy Lawrence

They used to charge bikes, cars, but not people, to go through the gate. There was a side gate where you could just walk through as pedestrians but if they opened the gate, they charged you. So a bicycle, you had to pay a penny. And they used to keep those gates closed and that also used to make sure the cattle didn't get out. The tollgates operated during the 1953 floods. But after that, no.

Alan Green

Cart to Colchester

Never been out of Wivenhoe I hadn't, when I was a child, because there was no buses those days, nothing at all. And when we went to Colchester, we used to have to go on a horse-drawn cart certain days and pay our fare to the driver of the cart. You caught the cart outside of the Greyhound. They did used to wash it out, but it was an open cart. But that was quite expensive. One side of the cart might be about four, other side about four, so they took about eight. Then you met in the High Street at Colchester after about a couple of hours, then they brought you home. That was supposed to be a really good day!

Ivy Knappett

Cedric's bus business

The person who started Cedric's bus business off was Cedric Peck. He was a bus driver and he had a twenty-five-seater, and he had it before the War and he ran it all the way through the War as well, and after the War! And he was quite a good character. He had four pumps there before the War. He drove everywhere. He took the local football team out to away matches. He took the cricket team out. And took people to London for the shows and away to the seaside.

Alan Green

Cedric Peck, that's the old man, he run a taxi service. And if you wanted him in the middle of the night like, say, childbirth or something like that, you'd go down to the house next to the garage, pull a bit of string and the bell would ring in his bedroom! Twice he's taken me into the maternity hospital. He was a nice old man, old Mr Peck. There's a house next to the garage, the family all lived in there, and his bedroom was above the front door, and it used to have a bit of string hanging down.

June Sansom

Coach outing with Cedric's to a London theatre, 1955; Sylvia Weatherall in centre. (Sylvia Weatherall)

As a kid I used to go down to 'the Pecks,' it wasn't called Cedric's! They lived in the old house, and they had a middle room which looked out over the garage. So I used to help out with the petrol pumps, but really, I went to watch the wrestling on the TV on a Saturday afternoon, because we didn't have a television and dad worked there anyway. Old Ceddie drove taxis for people in the village. Kath, his wife, I think she was the brains. [Later of their sons] Graham ran car repairs, while Ray was more to do with the coaches. But they all drove the coaches, like for school runs. [In the early fifties] I think they maybe had one coach or two, perhaps.

We'd do local runs in England, like a lot of runs to London from the University. And I did most of the European work for them – quite a lot of school trips, like Brightlingsea School. Three times I took them to France. And quite a lot of work from the Colchester Garrison, taking soldiers out, and they were going to the Moselle, wine tasting.

John Barton

Living by the railway

Living by the railway there was plenty of soot! We used to stand on the top of the bank in the summer and see all these trains full of trippers come down from London to Clacton. The old steam trains had all this soot, and the sparks used to come out and the railway banks used to catch fire, and we would have to keep throwing buckets of water on because you couldn't get the railway men right away.

Marjorie Goldstraw

Railway steam engine drivers

Working as a fireman and then driver on a variety of lines, and steam engine record-holder, Colin has lived in Wivenhoe from 1967.

It's a partnership, the driver uses the energy that the fireman produces, and if you haven't got a good fireman, then it's very hard work for the driver. The fireman would assist the driver with seeing signals, because with a large boiler in front of you, the driver's view was quite badly impaired from one side, so if the fireman knew the road very well, he could observe the signals on his side. And you'd fire the engine according to the gradients, so if you're on a downward incline, you ceased firing, because you didn't require so much steam, but when the engine had to work hard on rising gradients, then you used to have the fire prepared to cope with it. The driver was boss in those days! Drivers used to spend a long time learning the road – it's called 'road learning.' Diesels hadn't got the character, because no two steam engines perform quite the same. There was the risk too, if you didn't secure yourself in, you could even get thrown out the side of the locomotive, because they lurched and jumped a great deal – 150 tons hurtling along, jumping and banging around.

Colin Andrews

Railway tales

When I was [on duty] in London, I lived in a railway hostel at Ilford, it became quite a little village and collecting point, so when we moved this way I knew drivers from Clacton and Colchester, and some are our friends today. There was a guy they called the 'royal driver' – Fred Griffin – who was a very large fellow with a very shiny badge, very clean overalls, very smart, and felt that he had some kind of ultimate control over everything! And I always remember a driver at Stratford – his name was Bungay Will Torton, and his ambition was to suck all the papers off Witham bookstall, on the *Norfolkman*. And he achieved it! The story is that he was rostered on the *Norfolkman* for one week, and the newsagent at Witham was pretty well aware of the ambitions of a lot of the drivers – because as the trains pass through, they create a vacuum, it's in a cutting – so he used to get the shutters down early when he could hear the *Norfolkman* coming. On the Monday, Bungay was running a little bit late, and his fireman sounded the whistle, so the newsagent was pre-warned, and had the shutters down! But he got him on the Tuesday, he run about a minute or two early and warned his fireman not to sound the whistle – and he looked back and saw all the papers following down the line!

Colin Andrews

Schools and Education

Playtime

One thing that's a bit funny was that suddenly everybody would take a ball to school and we'd play ball, then everybody would take skipping ropes, and we'd all skip! And then it would be the cigarette cards. Then it was marbles. My mother used to buy me marbles and I used to take them to school and lose them all! I was no good at that! Then everybody would have spinning tops. But it's funny how suddenly everything changed and it would be something else.

Olive Whaley

Miss Smith and Miss Grasby

Miss Smith and Miss Grasby were two, in many ways, quite interesting characters. The combination of Smith and Grasby was peculiar. I'd better not use the word that I suspect about their relationship! But Miss Smith was definitely the dominant one.

Miss Grasby knew a lot about football, and she was very good at teaching boys. She had a very agreeable personality, quite a sense of humour, a musician, and she was well-liked.

Miss Smith was quite a battle-axe. She was angry, a grey-eyed monster, and she dominated! The children were afraid of her, the teachers were afraid of her. For instance there was a so-called 'staff room' which the staff never went into because Miss Smith made it entirely her office, so we ate our sandwiches in the classroom. And she ruled the children with an iron rod.

Tom Wiseman

Retirement of Miss Smith, Wivenhoe School head teacher, 29 April 1955. (John Stewart)

Punishing

A lot of people grumbled about Miss Smith. She was very very strict but I never knew her to be unfair. Talk about fierce! She had iron grey hair, done in earphones over her ears. She had an immaculate navy blue suit and a white shirt blouse with a big blue bow tie. She pranced up and down and she said, 'I am having things very different in this school. And if people don't behave they will be punished.'

But there were only two girls she ever smacked. One was a girl that she couldn't do much about because she was out of control. She was filthy, dirty, she stunk, honestly! And she was sat right the other side of the big hall there, she wasn't allowed to mix with anybody else, she wasn't allowed to go out to play when other people did. And the other girl lived near to where Miss Smith did and she was very very bright at maths. And Miss Smith let her go on doing far more advanced things than we did but she found out she was copying the answers out of the answer book! And she got smacked as well.

Freda Annis

Miss Smith, we used to call her 'Muggie.' She could be very sadistic. She had her cane and she used to use it. I had many a smack on the bum with that! And she gave me such a smack round the ear one day because I didn't know my tables! Can you imagine it today! My father went down that school he was absolutely furious! He said, 'If there's any ear'ole clipping to do, I will do it. And it will be you that's in the firing line.' So he said, 'Don't you ever lay a hand on either of my children ever again.' And she never did.

Sylvia Weatherall

Left-handed

My mother used to draw and paint and she taught me to read and write before I went to school. And I was left-handed, but that was a crime. They used to come round the classroom with a ruler, so she made sure that I used my right hand before I went to school. But I still can't throw a ball with my right hand and all games I had to play with my left.

Marjorie Goldstraw

Wivenhoe Boys' School

The Boys' School was where the library is now. Our lessons were totally different to what they are now. We were lucky here. We had woodwork and we had metalwork, we had book-binding – many of the crafts that they don't bother to teach nowadays. We used to have our PT in the playground! We used to have our sports day over on what is the King George V playing field now. There used to be the horticultural show every year and school sports. It was a typical village school. We had quite an assortment of lads, even some from the other side of the river came over on the ferry to school. Others used to come down from right up on the Clacton Road and they had to walk to school in those days. There was no school buses!

Mr Cater was the headmaster, he was a very very strict man but a very just man. I had the cane once and that was the only time I did have the cane! I was told to stop in because I hadn't done quite as much as he thought I might do. He said, 'You stay in for half an hour after school,' but there were two of us and we didn't. And the next morning we were up in front of all the school there and we had six of the best! I learnt my lesson!

It was not like it is now, at some schools that I have been to and heard pupils calling the teachers by their Christian name. That would not have gone down very well in those days! It would have been very much more caning, probably out of the door! But we knew our place.

Gilbert Whaley

Intercultural Broomgrove

Obviously, being close to the University we have a very strong – I use the phrase 'multi-cultural' but I'll also use the phrase 'intercultural,' because

I think there's two different aspects to our school. That's been one of the big things. Schools in Wivenhoe have a very mixed population in terms of children from other countries. At the moment I think we have children from Kuwait, Saudi Arabia, Russia, Mexico, America, and we've had children from Finland, Norway, France, Argentina, Japan, we have from China, from Hong Kong, and I don't think we've ever let the parents down.

Lyn Button

Colne, Colchester and Beyond

Refusing to go to Brightlingsea

Some of the older ones refused to go to the newly-opened, what would now be called the Secondary Modern, at Brightlingsea, which had a very chequered career in its early days. There was a good deal of stirring. The fishing villages which were strong in their community sense, the families were very loyal, supported each other, particularly in times of trouble. And the rivalry between Brightlingsea and Wivenhoe was strong, particularly when it came to football matches. They weren't matches, they were battles! So there was all this rivalry and [when the Brightlingsea school opened], I'm quite sure encouraged by Miss Smith and Miss Grasby, a group of stalwart families of the Wivenhoe community [went on] standing up for their rights. So arrangements were made for a group of about thirty pupils to stay at Wivenhoe School as a class of mixed seniors.

Tom Wiseman

Boarding school

I was here at holidays, and we had a big trunk which was sent off about four or five days before you went back to school and it was called 'PLA' – 'Passengers' Luggage in Advance.' We used to take it down to the station here and it went off and magically reappeared at school. I always enjoyed coming home, although I think one of the snags

of going to a boarding school is that you lose local friends and I think that's a pity.

Halcyon Palmer

Brightlingsea or Colchester: a class thing

For me, the Grammar School didn't enter into the discussion at all. I never thought about sitting the entrance exam. It was a class thing. We were a working-class family and you didn't really go to the Grammar School. It was the posh boys from the top end of the village who went to the Grammar School and the oiks from the bottom end of the village, if they were really clever and really lucky, they'd go to the Technical School. Or you went to Brightlingsea School and finished when you were fifteen.

Dennis Sparling

I was at Brightlingsea School and all those people who were going into work at the age of four-teen were called into the assembly hall. And our Headmaster got up and said, 'All you people are leaving,' and they gave us options of where to go to – shipyards, on the land (of which several went), the fishing industry, and Paxman's. And we all went our various ways, but the shipyards was very popular.

Charles Scofield

Churches

Wivenhoe's parish church, St Mary's, can be traced back to the early Middle Ages, and of the Nonconformists the Congregationalists first appeared in the seventeenth century, followed in the nineteenth century by the Swedenborgians and the Methodists, and most recently by the Roman Catholics. Our earlier memories come from the mid-twentieth century when the churches were central to everyday life for all ages; later memories show how they have been changing. Stephen Hardie was Rector 1976-92, David Thomas since then.

Church Life as Everyday Life

I went to St Mary's, morning and night. I was in the choir from the age of seven till about thirteen. I got 3/3d per quarter – that's for twelve or thirteen Sundays, twice a Sunday. A massive amount! And then we got paid a little bit extra for weddings. Mr Glozier was the choirmaster as well as the organist. We used to go one night a week to rehearse.

Alan Green

We had a bit of a celebration earlier this year, on Easter Sunday, because that was the fiftieth anniversary of my joining the church choir. 1954? I was nearly eight years old. There were a whole gang of us, all the local ruffians joined, so it was good fun. I remember going to sing at the launching of a couple of ships at Wivenhoe Shipyard. One was a minesweeper. Lots of people, and the Rector blessed the ship and we sang a couple of hymns – including *Eternal Father Strong to Save*!

Graham Wadley

Sea Harvest celebration at the Methodist Church, 1930s. (John Stewart)

I was a member of the St Mary's congregation as a young man, and in actual fact being footloose and fancy free at one particular time, I remember being in the pew behind this row of girls that stood in front of us, and thinking to myself, 'Mmm, she's nice piece of two, three and ten! I'll have to follow this up.' I gradually persisted until we got together as a courting couple, and we did eventually marry in 1951.

Walter Wix

We never went anywhere else

Once a year we used to have a Sunday school outing, to Walton. We used to go on the train, and they had streamers out, it was a real thing! For tea we used to go to the Congregational Hall at Walton. And we'd come back and we'd get a bag of nuts and an orange and a three corner pastry.

And that was a day – well, we never went out anywhere else.

Barbara Donohue

One man and his God

The people who used to go, of course, the Lovelesses sat in the middle aisle, and the churchwardens were Harry Thorpe, and Jimmy Moore, and at the end of every prayer you'd hear Jimmy Moore, he always used to say 'Aaaaaa-men!' in a very loud voice! What was different, though, was you went to church, you came out, you nodded to one or two people, but it was not a social event. It was one man and his God. Not like it is now where people congregate at the back of the church and have a cup of coffee! So it wasn't actually a church community as such.

Olive Whaley

Reverend R.H. Jack

Reverend Jack was a marvellous vicar. He was a remarkable man. He was a very tall man. He was Scots, actually, and he used to ride a very upright bike and when we first had a parish magazine he used to bring it round himself, and it was a penny. And he always used to seem to be at ours on a Friday afternoon and I said to him one day, 'Why do you always come on a Friday?' So he said, 'Shall I tell you something?' So I said, 'Yes.' So he said, 'Your mother has nice buns just out of the oven on a Friday, and I have a lovely cup of tea!' And I said, 'Oh! You naughty man!' And he laughed!

Freda Annis

Four years in the desert

Every year I grow trays of plants, which they have at the church, when they have their open day, and they sell them. David Thomas, the rector, he's very pleased. He said, 'Don't forget the plants, Phil.' Because I used to be in the choir, church choir. When I was abroad [in the war], I could always see that church, you know, in my mind, when I was in the desert. You never forget things at home, do you? I spent four years out there altogether, and in my mind always, the old church, yes…

Phil Faucheux

Ringing the changes

The Congregationalists were remarkable in having a very forceful woman minister as early as 1960-66, but all the churches were changing in different ways.

Rev Clementina Gordon

She was the reverend. When she came to live in Wivenhoe she came up in her boat. She used to ride round Wivenhoe on her horse. She used to drive an old minibus up to the new estates to collect all the children for Sunday school. She used to take the children on her boat. She was paramount in getting [the new church] built, she was the one that urged it on.

Patricia Coventry, Pat Moss and Barbara Donohue

Very refreshing

It was very refreshing to come to Wivenhoe. Because I was brought up in a very evangelical, fairly fundamentalist Methodist church up in rural Norfolk. There were a lot of things that I really questioned that I was uncomfortable to express. There's a body of people who say that the Bible is literally true from beginning to end, and I couldn't go along with that. I always had to weigh my experience with what was written in the Bible, and try and understand why and how.

The Methodist church in Wivenhoe was very refreshing. The building had been modernised. And because of the influence of the new university, it was also full of people who were much more questioning, more open, and more willing to experiment. And it still is.

Phil Bingham

Developing a musical tradition

[St Mary's] also has a very strong musical tradition. Our director of music and organist, Graham Wadley, is very very good indeed, very highly regarded, and he's developed, over time, a very good choir and a very strong musical tradition. And what he does on certain occasions in the year, like Good Friday evening, is to invite choir members from other churches – Coggeshall, Sudbury, Harwich – to come and share, and to do, say, part of the *Messiah*, and that also happens with summer canticles and also at remembrance time. Very high quality music in a local church, which people much enjoy – not only locally, people come from quite far afield to appreciate the music.

Rev David Thomas

Graham Wadley at the organ of St Mary's, 1970s. (Graham Wadley)

Run down

My predecessor had been Douglas Gaye, and he had been quite an elderly man when he arrived and I think seventy-three or more when he left. He'd been a colonel of two different regiments, and he trained for the ministry very late in life. Very much a gentleman, very much of the old school. But I think it's not unfair to say that by the time I arrived there the church was very run-down. And that's always a good thing. I always say to my curates, 'Don't accept the offer of going to a church that is a rip-roaring success because it can only go downhill whilst you're there. Go to a church that needs picking up and you might be able to pick it up a bit, and that's good.'

Canon Stephen Hardie

Work in the church

Wivenhoe church it had the advantage and disadvantage of not having a good church hall. Because we didn't have a good church hall, I did persuade

Congregational church event. (Congregational church)

Joan Hickson, Miss Marple. (Kitty Funnel)

people to make some changes within the building. They were controversial when it happened, because we took some of the pews out – we did put them back again – but they were made moveable, and the floor was carpeted, and it was possible to have tables and put the pews against the tables, and we would eat in the church. [We made a small] kitchenette at the back of church, and also, we fitted two loos in the porch.

At that time we had living in the parish, and very close to the church, Joan Hickson the actress. People, of course, knew her from the television as 'Miss Marple.' I know she was a good actress, but as far as Miss Marple was concerned she didn't have to act, that's what she was like all the time. She dressed like that and she spoke like that all the time. And I used to visit her quite often, she always liked me to come at around half past five or six so she could offer me a sherry.

So when we had this work done in the church I kept her in the picture and she just said, politely and nicely, that she didn't approve. When it was all finished I said, 'Now, Joan, I know you don't approve of what's happened, but I would like to take you over and show you now it's finished.' So I took her over to church and she saw the area where

the pews had been put back, now over carpet, and I showed her the kitchen unit which looks quite like a vestments' chest until you open it up and find that there's a sink underneath and work surfaces and loads of plugs to heat urns. And then I showed her the new loos in the south porch. And she said, 'Mmm, yes. I must say it's all very good but you know, my dear, people have managed without lavatories in churches for thousands of years!'

Canon Stephen Hardie

Faith journeys

I felt it was a very strong community that had quite a lot of change. I felt that the continuity is sometimes a strength and so I've preferred to work on building up the faith rather than changing the structure in which the faith is worshipped. By being available to people, offering occasional services to people at critical points in their lives, preparing people for baptism, preparing people for marriage, and supporting, befriending people when their relatives die. It doesn't mean to say they're going to pour into the church on Sunday, but it is to offer them the friendship and support and help of the church at that point in time. And many people have joined the church as a result, but that's for them to choose.

Listening to people's faith journeys, or struggles in their faith journeys, is important to them, and to me. And listening to people, in pubs or in shops, in the street – I always allow myself an extra twenty minutes to enable a conversation to happen, if you happen to meet up there, because I like to be available to people, to give time to people. I like, also, to be around for all the major community activities as well, whether it's the May Fair, or the June Market, or the Regatta, or Jazz on the Quay, just to be around. I find people find it easier to talk to me in their familiar places – whether it's the Co-op, or the pub. Many of them do come and talk to me specifically about something in the house. I might visit their home as well.

Rev David Thomas

six

Societies
and Clubs

Wivenhoe Allotment and Gardens Association Show. (Peter Duffield)

Societies

Wivenhoe is reputed to have over a hundred active socie-
ties — a very remarkable number for its size — so that
these memories touch mainly on the most long-standing
and largest groups. They range from the newer performing
societies to the earlier sports clubs, and there is the Sailing
Club too, which we will come to later. All these societies
thrive on the support of still larger numbers of activists.

People who do things

Everybody knows her as Penny Lear because she
had the hairdressers, but she's really Penny Kraft
– and she did a booklet of *Wivenhoe At Your Service*,
and I think she counted up there are about seventy
or eighty groups of activities in Wivenhoe – people
who do things. There's the Scouts and the Guides
and the Brownies, and the Rainbows and Beavers,
and that's just one little portion. There's all the acting,
the players, panto, youth theatre, the Gilbert and
Sullivan Society. There's the folk club. And they're
only the ones that I know. There is lots of painting,
the Art on the Railing... There's a Sugarcraft Group.
There's ladies' groups, there's women's guilds. There
are the churches as well, they're all in the different
things that they have involved. There's yoga, there's
line dancing, there's a Pilates group – and they're
only the ones that I can think of.

Linda Edwardson

Wivenhoe Carnival

We were on the committee. Towards the end, the
Carnival route used to go from the Park, go out, up
Manor Road – that was fun! Over to Vine Farm,
through there, then down on to Parkwood Avenue
and go in at the top of the Park. Used to sometimes
take us about two hours to get all the way round
there. Several of the associations took part. But that
just got less and less. I think the reason was money.
Because the day that they have the June market we
used to shut the village down the bottom and all the
associations could have stalls all along the road, then
the police started charging to close the road! They

charged us about £200 to go up Manor Road. Well,
we weren't making that kind of money.

Peter and Diane Duffield

A community of people

We had some wonderful evenings, Hollywood
night, the Forties night, the Bunker party. Really,
since the year 2000, and doing all these things, we
realised that there was a community of people in
Wivenhoe that were prepared to haul themselves
out and have a good time and raise much much
money for many many many charities. There's a
group of people that continuously get together to
do certain things, albeit that we're all dancing and
singing and drinking and eating, doing it, but at
the end of the day, we've raised money for so many
things and had a good time doing it.

Carol Green

St John Ambulance

As a child I can remember being involved with
the St John Ambulance group in Wivenhoe. Ruth
Munson [a Wivenhoe teacher] used to run a cadet
section and I can only remember girls being there.
We used to go along each week and she would
instruct us on first aid, and we had to wear a uniform and we had to be very smart and have very
clean shoes and very smart clean dresses, etc., and
she used to enter us into a regional competition
each year, and we were forever winning because
she was such a good teacher!

Helen Douzier

Mum and I were members of the St John Ambulance
Brigade. We used to go down there once a week
and learn how to mend broken bones and save
people's lives. And they used to go and spend time
on Clacton seafront, looking after people. I think
the day I did it we had one donkey bite and two
bee stings, or two wasp stings, and a cut foot! I

St John Ambulance, retirement of Mrs Ruth Munson, presentation by Joyce Blackwood, 1950s. (Joyce Blackwood)

guess I must have just started the senior school then, between the ages of about nine and thirteen.

Pat Alston

There's only seven of us in there now, the women. There's no girl cadets now, and I can't see the young girls of today wanting to take that interest like we used to love going in for cup competitions.

Pat Green

Scouts and Guides

We were meeting down at the Infants' School and it wasn't really satisfactory because we weren't allowed to scratch the floor, had to wear plimsolls for meetings. And so I had a word with our chairman, Billy Cracknell, and said, 'We ought to see if we could find somewhere to have our own Headquarters.' So we hunted high and low for a piece of ground and couldn't find any, and then Billy Cracknell suggested that we approach the Guides to see if they'd like to come in with us. Well, I was a Scout leader and my wife was the Guide Captain. So it was a difficult job to approach the Guides!

Well eventually we put in the paper that we were looking for a piece of land to build a Scout Headquarters and a gentleman went round and saw Billy Cracknell and offered him a piece of land which was full of trees, behind the council offices – for twenty-five pounds. After that, we had to clear the ground, that was full of trees. We all chipped in, took the trees down and then eventually we had all the roots pulled out. Then Les Kemble was approached, and he designed the headquarters and oversaw the building of it, which was done by tradesmen but not builders as such, so it didn't go through books for creaming off the profits. And it's in the hands of Scouting and Guiding in Wivenhoe for posterity – which is good.

Alan Green

Colne Social Club and the Masons

Colne Lodge of the Freemasons was founded in 1893, and its Masonic Hall built in 1911.

The Colne Social Club started at the end of the First World War. It wasn't built as a snooker place at all, it was built as a social club, a reading room.

Tony Forsgate

There was the men's social club – the Colne Social Club – which was in Park Road, but it wasn't necessarily for working-class men. It was slightly more elite. And, of course, the other very strong thing in the village was the Masonic Lodge. Again, it tended to be the more affluent and the higher echelon of people who were white-collar workers, rather than dirty hands workers in the shipyards.

Dennis Sparling

Three generations

I've got tremendous respect for my father. Involved in so much. Very sporty. Sailing Club, Cricket Club, and Bowls Club, and left them all fairly well, I think. Yes, very popular chap. He was a trustee of the Masonic Hall for many many years. Very active up the Masonic Hall. Because I went in at twenty-one years of age, jumped the queue because of my father's commitment, and I was the third generation of Masons in Wivenhoe. Not been beaten before. My grandfather, my father, and then myself, and we've been through the chair and became Master of the Lodge and done our bit. I think we've contributed to Wivenhoe, on the charity side, quite well. You used to have to be a sea captain, or an owner, or a business person, years ago, but now I'm very pleased, anybody can come along and join. And we have a wonderful Lodge up there, it's well received and very supportive. I think the present membership is [about ninety]. And they respected the sea and that's why we only meet from September to May. We don't meet in the summer because the yachtspeople couldn't get there, because they were away.

Charles Scofield

You get to know people when you belong to the Masons, you get to be able to depend on people. As a Mason, moving into a different area, you are immediately among friends.

Len Drinkell and Brian Heasman

The Foresters and the Masons

I was put into the Foresters when I was a young man, about fourteen or fifteen, and they used to meet at the Park Hotel. That's the Manchester Unity. A lot of the oldish men were in it. But the Masons have got their building next door to the Methodist chapel. They were all there last night, with their motor cars!

It's called the Colne Lodge. Well, we jokingly say they're responsible for putting a lot of square pegs in round holes! It's not what you know but who you know. But people who are Masons, who are working-class, they are more a true Mason. The whole idea of Masons was to help your fellow man.

Don Smith and Pat Ellis

Performing Arts

While local music, especially in the churches and the pubs, goes back a long way, the present flourishing of the performing arts is new in Wivenhoe. The Wivenhoe Players were formed in 1968, the Youth Theatre in 1994, the Folk Club in the 1970s, and the Pantomime and the Gilbert and Sullivan Society in the 1980s.

Drama

Astonishing creativity

I've mixed an awful lot with theatre people, I've always been a snob really. Afterwards, coming here I realised in Wivenhoe there is an astonishing creativity in amateur things. I mean, *Twelfth Night*, I'd never seen such a lovely production of it. And I've never seen such a charming, delightful Maria and Sir Toby and Sir Andrew were absolutely glorious. It really opened my eyes to how creative amateur stuff can be and I've started to look at it in quite a different way. I've certainly never seen amateur productions like the ones they put on in Wivenhoe – so creative, so bursting with energy.

Leila Berg

Drama group

When I was a child my mother used to put on pantomimes and they used to put on little musical shows at the old Boys' School. I used to be in the pantomimes as a child! And I can remember Lil and Cyril Brown. He used to run the men's hairdressers and his wife used to do all the make-up for the Drama Group. They used to go to Severalls Hospital, which was then a hospital for mental patients, and they used to go and perform for them at Christmas.

Helen Douzier

Wivenhoe Players

It was Lady Clare Abrahall who started the Players. She must have been in her sixties to seventies, and she was a wonderful character. She had worked, during the First World War, as a driver for a major who was busy inventing the parachute, and he used to do parachute drops all round the country, and she used to go and collect him when he landed, and she used to tell us tales about this, in the Black Buoy. She had her own seat in the Black Buoy, and a little dachshund called 'Winkle,' who nestled under her chair. She had a very gravelly voice. She did smoke a pipe as well. But she directed a lot of the Players first productions, and she wrote some of them. She wrote a famous piece called *The Butler in the Box*, and was the founding mover of the Wivenhoe Players [in 1968], and along with Molly Beeson, who also directed many of the early productions.

It was mainly local people, but their technical support was drawn from the University, the electrician at the University, and John [my future husband], who was a student there, was doing a lot of technical theatre at the University as well. In 1974, when we got married, and I first came to Wivenhoe, I did help with the Players productions, and John was very much involved in the technical side. But my involvement with the Players, as a director, came later.

Sheila Foster

Wivenhoe Players production of Blithe Spirit, *late 1970s. (Marcel Glover)*

Blithe Spirit

The first show I did in Wivenhoe was *Blithe Spirit*, with the Wivenhoe Players. Phyllis Richardson was playing Elvira in grey make-up and grey diaphanous clothes, playing a ghost, it was wonderful. She is one of the founding members. *Blithe Spirit* is quite a technical play because the last scene you have the spirit of Elvira throwing things about the stage. When I gave the Players the schedule it had the technical rehearsal and the dress rehearsals all timed into it and they said, 'What is a technical rehearsal?' because they hadn't had one before. And I was shocked and horrified and I told them what a technical rehearsal was and they said, 'Yes, but we only do this for fun! You're trying to pretend it's a professional thing.' I was very pompous because I thought I'd been taught how to do everything properly and I thought, 'How can they possibly contemplate not doing it my way?' So we had the technical rehearsal and we had people there till midnight and then having to go and catch trains to London the next morning. I did have to learn, over the years, to unbend a little.

Sheila Foster

Shakespeare in the garden

Ted and Hally Palmer's garden itself is magical and it weaves its own spell over the show that goes on there. They have been wonderful hosts to us and we have done three plays there now. In *A Midsummer Night's Dream* Moonshine is represented by a man with a bush and a dog, and we had little Carl – Ray Bowen's daschund – he came and actually stole that scene every night with his rather beautiful sad-looking eyes! And then with *Much Ado* we decided we had to top that, so we had the messenger arriving on a horse. It was quite dramatic and we were loaned the horse, very kindly, by Robina Taplin. The horse was good fun and we had a rota of people who had to go round with a dustpan and brush following the horse, so that there was not too much left on the stage afterwards that shouldn't have been. That was quite a highlight.

Sheila Foster

Youth Theatre

The Youth Theatre ran, and still does run, for two weeks every summer and we do our main production then. The kids who were in the first tranche, if you like, for instance, Kevin West, he's gone on to train as an actor, and Dan Shearer who directed *Midsummer Night's Dream*, he's just finished a directing course at RADA. Three of our current members, so that's three people just from a small group like ours, have gone on to join the National Youth Theatre!

Sheila Foster

Wivenhoe Pantomime

The first pantomime was in 1989. It was only when Peter Kerr arrived in the village, with scripts that he'd written, and keen, also, to start a pantomime. We rehearsed it, and it went on in the January of 1990. Peter Kerr wrote and directed, and rehearsed above the Greyhound – in the good tradition of the Wivenhoe Players, who always rehearsed above the Greyhound at the time. So that was the beginning of the Pantomime Group.

Sheila Foster

Our problem is that there's the University just up the road and, when we were talking about putting on *Peter Pan* people think of Peter Pan flying, and there is no way that you can do any flying in the William Loveless Hall, it's not high enough. So people were saying, 'Well, why don't we take it to the Lakeside Theatre at the University?' But we say, 'No, we are Wivenhoe. The Pantomime Group is the *Wivenhoe* Group.' I think Wivenhoe is a unique place in that we're four miles from Colchester, but we are a very separate entity and we like it that way!

Linda Edwardson

The Pageant

I directed the Pageant in St Mary's in 1985/86. And that was a whole community show. Robin Close wrote that. It was based on the local book by Olive Whaley, *The Day Before Yesterday*. It was the factual history of Wivenhoe and particularly centred on the church history. So we had different groups of people from various bits of Wivenhoe. For instance, the Bowen family rehearsed a theme which was about a family – husband and wife and two sons. We had some spectaculars that everybody got involved in, like the beginning of the railways where all the children became the railway, going up the centre of the aisle! And we had people being different households dotted round the church and then all dropping like flies at a certain given point! A dramatic history!

Sheila Foster

Loveless problems

When the William Loveless Hall was built, whenever it was, 1960s, I don't think they envisaged the theatre side of Wivenhoe taking off. So to put on a production in the William Loveless Hall we have to actually build the stage. There are big units which are housed somewhere behind the council offices and these have to be brought down to the hall – manhandled, carried by at least two or three people – and then put together like a jig-saw puzzle and bolted together, and that's two or three

Wivenhoe Pantomine, Queen of the Pirate Isle*, 1992. (Marcel Glover)*

hours work just to put that staging in. And then you have to build the sets on top of that.

Linda Edwardson

Music and song

Folk Club

We started up a little folk club up at The Arts Club. Then the Arts Club closed down, so in 1981 we moved down an outbuilding at the back of the Station Hotel. We'd get a barrel of beer, and we had various singers. That started off a little folk club, which eventually moved to the Greyhound.

Celia Hirst

Peter Kerr actually ran a Folk Club in Wivenhoe – I think at the Cricket Club and various other venues – ages ago. I was born in South Africa, and moved to Crawley, and we did quite a lot of anti-apartheid things in Crawley, boycotting South African goods. I went to some guitar classes, and started singing with two other students, and we

were a trio – Ron, Rod and Joan! And very bad! We went round little Folk Clubs in the area, in the sixties there were a lot of Folk Clubs. But when we moved to Wivenhoe about the end of 1991, I knew one or two people here, one was Peter Kerr. [So they re-launched the Folk Club in 1992.]

We've had some very well known people. Shortly after we started it I met Martin Carthy at a festival and I was telling him we'd just started this little club in Wivenhoe and he said, 'Would you like me to come as a guest?' And I said, 'Don't be silly, Martin! We can't afford you!' And he said, 'Of course you can. I will come for a percentage of the door.' And I said, 'But we only charge £2 and £3 and it's not a very big room.' He said, 'That doesn't matter.'

Joan Gifford

Gilbert and Sullivan

[Janet and I] met at a party. I do remember after what feels like two glasses of sherry, that we found that we had this common interest [in Gilbert and Sullivan], and I said, 'You weren't brought up in Sevenoaks, were you?' And [Janet] said, 'No, the

Wivenhoe Gilbert and Sullivan Society, Patience, *1982: Stephen Hardie in front. (Janet Turner)*

Wivenhoe Gilbert and Sullivan Society, Iolanthe, *1983. (Janet Turner)*

Persian Gulf, which is just as bad!' And then I said, 'There doesn't seem to be any G & S around here,' and [she] said, 'No. And something should be done about it!' And that was a very key phrase, in my mind. And so we did!

At the time Stephen Hardie was the rector. And I had been hearing him sing in church and nudged my husband and said, 'He might be useful as Strephon or something like that.' And we did nobble him and say, 'Would you ever be interested in singing G & S?' And he said, 'Oh yes, I have done things like that in the past.' And so little by little we asked people.

We invited people to my house, people that we knew were interested, and we had a sing-song, some of the best bits of *Iolanthe,* and we asked different people to sing solo parts. And at the end, somebody said, 'Well, surely we're not going to leave it there!' And then you and I said, well, obviously *Trial by Jury* would be the best one to kick off with, because it's the simplest. It's three-quarters of an hour, and it's like a little concert performance, there's no action in it. But it's got the most fiendish chorus so we started out quite ambitiously in that respect. We got a number of students that year, didn't we? And we put this on in the church, and it was one night only, 50p entrance, wasn't it!

Clare Durance with Janet Turner

One of the activities that I was very involved with was the Wivenhoe Gilbert and Sullivan Society which was very cheerful, very active bearing in mind that everybody there was totally amateur. The William Loveless Hall stage was not exactly brilliant, and really, with a lot of love and energy I think they were rather good productions. Certainly the people who were part of them thoroughly enjoyed them. I always sang a principal baritone or bass part. I was never a good dancer, a stage mover, that was never my strength. They were a really good group of people, interesting people. There was something very Wivenhoe about the group as well – very open to talk about things, rejoicing in the diversity of all the people who were members.

Canon Stephen Hardie

I think it would be very much harder to get [a Gilbert and Sullivan Society] off the ground now if you started from nowhere, because we have found it difficult to get younger people in. I think when we were in our thirties it seemed less difficult to go out in the evening and sing. I think people now, of that age group, both of them are working, they're absolutely whacked at the end of the day. Once they've put their children to bed all they want to do is flop, and if they do go out they tend to go out to eat or out to the flicks, but they don't want to go out and do something like this. And I think a lot of them regard it as slightly mad anyway, and more for the elderly!

Clare Durance

Barbershop

We went up to the Arts Club and formed this group, singing American barbershop. It was fascinating! And from nothing that went on to quite a high standard for a good number of years. There was about ten or so, and we used to travel the county appearing at different venues – usually with a pub at the end of it. I also remember, with some amusement, our best engagement of the year was always with the Hard of Hearing Club from Frinton! And the only sad point in our little careers was that we came to the Horse & Groom in Wivenhoe, and we were kindly asked to leave because we were making too much noise and disturbing the regulars! But, in fact, they didn't mind at all!

Bill Heslop

Jazz trio, 1960: trumpet, Black Buoy landlord Roy Cabuschier; guitar, Dave Weatherall; piano, Alan Woodhurst. (Dave Weatherall)

Dancing

We formed a little Old Tyme Dance Club down in the British Legion. There was quite a few regulars. My wife introduced me to old tyme dancing and we used to have great fun! We used to have a little dance band come sometimes, a trio of piano, drums and violin. But in the main we had a record player – I've still got loads of seventy-eight records, old tyme dances – Harry Davidson and Sidney Thompson.

Gilbert Whaley

The Legion, they used to hold dances. And the Foresters Hall, which was the holy of holies, some rather select crowds had dances there. I didn't go there till I was quite grown up but it wasn't a patch on the old Legion, not for fun and that sort of thing! Usually Saturday nights they used to have a dance at the Legion. And it was very well run. There were two men and their wives used to serve just biscuits and lemon and orange drinks, and these two men always used to be there at the door and if anybody was the worse for drink they'd throw them out! We did the foxtrot, waltzes. The Palais Glide! And the Veleta. And that was the highlight of our week. And that's how I really met Vic, because there'd be a crowd come from Brightlingsea, there'd be a crowd come from all over the place.

Freda Annis

The Engine Shed: key to the future

I would like to see a venue that might eventually become a sort of local Snape Maltings, that has a reputation for putting on work by visiting artists, by travelling theatre, travelling opera, as well as the local performing groups. So the Engine Shed is not just about Wivenhoe, it's helping to bring people into Wivenhoe. There's economic benefits that if you come here to Wivenhoe to see an Art Exhibition, then maybe you'll go and use the local shops. So it's part of a bigger picture as far as I'm concerned, that's why I'm passionate about the Engine Shed. The Engine Shed is the key to the future of Wivenhoe, otherwise the danger is we're a pleasant dormitory town…

Peter Hill

Sports Clubs

Cricket and bowls have both been played in Wivenhoe since the late eighteenth century. The present Cricket Club goes back to 1840, and the Bowls Club was founded in 1934, both appealing to leading people in the village. More plebian, football was reported from the 1890s, and the Wivenhoe Town Football Club formed in 1907. In a later phase they played as Wivenhoe Rangers, reverting to their original name in 1974. Although for a brief and very successful phase the footballers were financially backed by David Watts of the Port, all three clubs have relied basically on volunteer support. And for all three, securing a good long term ground has been crucial. The Football Club had particular difficulties, playing for many years on the sloping King George V Playing Fields.

Bowls

An old man's game?

FH: You may hear it said, that bowls is an old man's game. It is a young man's game, which older people are allowed to play.

CS: My father was the president at the time and my grandfather was dead against ladies joining, and we lived with my grandfather and he wouldn't have ladies up there, and that caused a bit of a confusion! But when [in 1946] that went through, he accepted it. There's a lot of the elderly members, don't take to the ladies.

FH: It seems to have continued even to this day, the men don't enjoy playing with the ladies. And I think there's a reason behind that, and it's fairly obvious. They don't like being beaten by the ladies!

CS: They're a tremendous asset, the ladies. You can't do without them. The ladies used to do all the teas.

Frank Hodgson and Charles Scofield

Wivenhoe Bowls Club: Frank Hodgson bowling. (Frank Hodgson)

Cricket

Gentlemen Presidents

Prior to going in the Army all the gentry were the president of the Cricket Club, president of the Football Club. So when we came out of the Army we were like all youngsters, we were bit of rebels to be honest. There was myself, and Len Drinkell. We wanted to play Sunday cricket so they had the AGM, which was held in the Boys' School, and we proposed Sunday cricket. Well, in those days two or three of the people who wanted Sunday cricket and played cricket, one was the chauffeur for the local doctor and they all had jobs with these people who owned positions in the Cricket Club in a presidential manner. So naturally they were scared to vote for Sunday cricket so we lost the vote! But, rebels that we were, the next AGM, we put forward a motion that the vote go by ballot! This was passed, so when the ballot came we had Sunday cricket! But the pure gentlemen that they were they resigned from the Cricket Club and shew their true mettle. But we got our Sunday cricket and moved on. If you can think of cricket, the gentry done the spin bowling, and the poor old fast bowler was the chap from down below! Well, that's a fact, isn't it?

Peter Sainty

Grammar School backbone

The Grammar School was the backbone of the club for members. That's where you learned about cricket.

Len Drinkell

One of the points about playing cricket at Wivenhoe when I was in my late teens/early twenties, was that out of the eleven who were playing, ten were Grammar School boys or ex-Grammar School boys, and the eleventh was a Boys' County High School. I think that's really because the Grammar School was a cricket and rugby school, whereas Brightlingsea were football, and there wasn't as much expertise on the cricket side in the Secondary Modern as there was in the Grammar School. The Grammar School had beautiful playing fields, well provided, all the equipment you needed, so consequently we had a good grounding in all of those sports.

Tony Forsgate

Two teams and a gramophone

They had two teams – the First XI. The first team would be away and the second team would be at home and we used to play all the villages – Elmstead, Kelvedon, Colchester and East Essex, sometimes a club at Ipswich – and old Cedric Peck, he had a twenty-five-seater coach so we used to hire that and go out in the coach when we played away. There was very little social life. We used to hold an open air dance in the cricket ground. We didn't have a live band, just a gramophone. Had a gentleman who ran that for us – he used to put it on a loud speaker. And the ladies would make cakes and tea and all that sort of thing, so they were jolly good evenings out the dances were.

Phil Faucheux

Mums and teas

As we got older I actually got quite into the scoring side of things. I think perhaps the lad who was

Wivenhoe Cricket Club, 1960s: Graham Wadley, captain, with Tony Forsgate seated on left with bat. (Tony Forsgate)

the scorer might have been the attraction originally – and I won't mention his name! I used to sit with the scorers and then eventually I did do the scoring sometimes. Oh, we used to just go off for a little walk and pick flowers by the allotments. But it was a very laid-back sort of day. We had rows of deckchairs and the mums all had their knitting, and there might be dogs or younger children that we could play with, very innocent pleasures!

The mums and the wives all had a rota for the teas, so we had to do that two or three times a year. The teas used to come up from the bakery in the village, and this huge cardboard box would appear with all the ingredients for tea and then it was the two ladies' jobs to put it together. So they'd work out whether it was going to be cheese and tomato, cheese and cucumber, or whatever, and have it all ready for them. And they used to have fabulous teas! Lots of different varieties of sandwich, and different fancy cakes, and things like tea breads and currant loaves, and then massive pots of tea!

Hilary Harvey

The Cricket fete and bowling for the pig

[From the 1950s] we always had the fete on the last Sunday in June. The whole club, everybody joined in, everybody helped. The highlight was the inter-pub darts tournament in the marquee. That used to bring all the men up. And if the men came, the wives came too. And then in the evening, an open air dance. We'd have lots of side shows and stalls and attractions. Rifle range, piano-smashing competition, donkey derby, boxing. Bowling for the pig – great organisation had to take place there. Because there was only one person ever won bowling for the pig, and that was Charlie Tayler. So you had to make sure you kept him off there, until late in the afternoon, because if he came along and got a high score, nobody else bothered.

Tony Forsgate, Roger Bacon, and Len Drinkell

They had the Cricket Fete every year, which raised a lot of money, and they had side shows and stalls, that was really good. I used to aim for the pony rides, every year, and I spent more money on there than anybody else! And the Duttons always used to have a turkey barbecue! In those days you didn't get burgers and things at all, so we just used to have these enormous crispy rolls with turkey in and it was fabulous! I suppose it was more like a hog roast but it was turkey because they had a turkey farm on the Alresford Road. They used to cook them on spits there and then slice the meat off and pack it into the rolls. They had coconut shy, bowling for the pig, the goldfish in the bag with the table tennis balls. Things like raffles – 'Guess the name of the doll.' And I suppose it must have been the early Sixties, quite adventurous, they used to get canned fizzy drinks, so fizzy lemonade and shandy. They had children's sports, races, tug of war, and then quite often, in the evening, they'd have some music and dance!

Hilary Harvey

The Cricket Club ground

Our garden backing onto the ground, I was always there. I love cricket. There was a toss-up whether the Football Club would get that land, or the Cricket Club. There was a lovely old lady, name of Kent, lived in Belle Vue Road, and she loaned the Cricket Club enough money to buy the land, and it had to be paid back with no interest. And I paid the last instalment.

Phil Faucheux

Football

Fierce with their umbrellas

There was a lot of inter-rivalry between football. Football, in Wivenhoe, was quite a big thing. Matches between Wivenhoe and Rowhedge and that were real – the ladies were very very fierce

with their umbrellas! They were really something! And Wivenhoe Rangers had quite a following. I can remember seeing two or three double-decker buses going away when they played away!

Don Smith

Wivenhoe Rangers

When I played with the Wivenhoe Rangers, on the breast pockets of our shirts we had a daffodil. Now, the Amos Charity Cup which Wivenhoe Rangers won five years in a row, after the third win, as Blake Amos was a horticulturalist, he had this daffodil, which amongst other things he was producing, and he named this daffodil the 'Wivenhoe Ranger.' Hence the hand-sewn daffodil, and they were hand-sewn by Mrs Cook in Park Road on each of our shirts.

Peter Green

Charity Challenge Cup

The Wivenhoe Charity Cup Committee was running after the War. There was a Cup awarded – the Wivenhoe Charity Challenge Cup – and it was for football mainly but a group of us, we got together after the War and we found a lot of old people living on their own deserved to have something for

Wivenhoe Town Football Club, 1930s. (John Stewart)

Christmas. So we played darts matches in different pubs all over the place in Wivenhoe, raised money. We had the Challenge Cup to be played for by the football teams so they were all invited to compete for it and the money we raised was spent on building up Christmas parcels so every old lady or gentleman in Wivenhoe over the age of seventy received a little bottle of brandy, butter, tea, probably a small Christmas pudding, tins, fruits... Well, that died out. Things do, don't they. Wivenhoe was growing.

Phil Faucheux

Football grounds

The Football Club had no definite ground, although they had a ground at the back of the Horse & Groom which is all built on now. And Wivenhoe Athletic used to play on what they call 'Spion Kop,' which is between Ernest Road and Stanley Road, there was all open field there. So there were two teams. They also played football on the Vine Farm Estate, which is all built up now, there was a field there. I remember playing football on the King George V Playing Field, and the charity cup always held our games there.

Phil Faucheux

In the late 1980s David Watts, the managing director of Wivenhoe Port, managed to buy Wivenhoe Town Football Club and put a lot of money into it. It achieved some good successes in the football scene. With the dwindling activities of Wivenhoe Port in the late eighties, David put less money in, until in 1994 he stopped putting money in at all. I arrived to the Town Council meeting to discover the council chamber full of Football Club supporters, to come and plead with the Town Council to see if we could do something to save the ground [off Elmstead Road].

David Watts wanted to sell the ground. He wanted a quarter of a million pounds, which is what he felt the site was worth; we felt it was worth a lot less than that. The Football Club, before I got involved,

had approached the Borough Council for financial support and the Borough Council said they couldn't put money into something which was partly a trading enterprise – because the Football Club was a semi-professional team, people were being paid. So I turned the thing round and with Geoff Langston, who was then Chairman of the Football Club, we approached the Borough Council and said, 'If we create a Charitable Sports Trust as an umbrella body to acquire the ground, and Wivenhoe Town Football Club continues to promote the idea of a semi-professional football team playing league football in one of the junior leagues, what would your reaction be?' Eventually we got some feedback, that if we could make it more than just football we would stand a better chance. So I spoke to the Tennis Club, who were looking around for a site, and we worked up a scheme with the Borough Council where they acquired the freehold of the land and we raised the money – six of us in Wivenhoe put some money in together, the Football Supporters Club put some money in, and the University put some money in. And we did a deal, actually here in the dining room of Toad Hall, with David Watts, where he finally accepted a sum, approximately half of his original price that he was asking for.

Peter Hill

Allotments and the Horticultural Shows

The Allotments

The Wivenhoe Allotment Holders Association was formed in 1931. Phil Faucheux was its secretary from 1959 until 1976.

A man's a man

There was a flourishing Allotment Association. They would tend to do their work on a Sunday morning, and after the allotment they would repair to the Horse & Groom pub at Wivenhoe Cross, which always used to have Adnams Ale and was always a good place for a drink. And you would get retired city stockbrokers and retired firemen, and a man's man. There was no class distinction of people not mixing with people of a different background. It was amazing.

Canon Stephen Hardie

Fighting along with old Major Tom

There was a threat from the old Urban District Council that we were going to lose our plots. We were all ex-servicemen, remember, a lot of us had just come back from the War. And we were determined to carry on with our allotments if we could. And then along came the Vine Farm, they started to build that, 1959/1960, and they put a sewer main right across the allotments into Field Way. So Major Tom Burt, he was the major-domo of the 22nd SAS, and they were stationed in Wivenhoe Park, and he was a very keen gardener, old Major Tom. He and I got together and he said, 'Look, Phil, we've got to do something about this. I think we might be losing our allotments.'

Well, the council wouldn't give us a direct answer about it. But coming through the allotments with their sewer main they had to dig a great big trench which destroyed several of the plots, so Tom and I took them to task and they had to put back the damage. I wrote to Julian Ridsdale who was our MP at the time, he lived at St Osyth Priory and he was a lovely fellow, he was a smashing old boy. So Julian Ridsdale came and I showed him over the allotments, and he said, 'Look, there's no reason for you to fear of getting your allotments taken over. What I want you to do now,' he said, 'is to write a letter to Lord Sandford.' So I said, 'Good heavens! Really?' He said, 'Yes, there's a new ministry being formed called the "Ministry of Environment" under Harold MacMillan's government. You write this letter and give him all the details and he will deal with it.' Well, I got a letter back from Lord Sandford's secretary telling us that action had been taken. The next thing I knew we'd got 'Security of Tenure' for ten years. That's all those years ago, and we're still there.

Phil Faucheux

Phil Faucheux and friend on allotment. (Phil Faucheux)

Vegetables in season

Dad had a twenty-rod plot – five and a half yards square, a rod. Quite a big piece of ground. And we'd grow enough cabbages, probably lasted all through the year. And runner beans in season. Dad used to bottle the runner beans, put them down in salt, slice them up, because there were no freezers in those days. We always grew enough potatoes to last us right through until they came again. The shed was always full of potatoes. The parsnips and carrots you could keep in the soil. We used to have some hard winters in those days.

It's a going concern. We've got a heck of a lot of power now, in the membership. We had our AGM last Sunday week and there were fifty-odd people turned up. We've got going on 600 members. And when I mean members, that's families, because there might be just a man as a member but the whole family rely on the plot as well. I would say there's going on for 110 plots now because we split a lot up. It's not everybody wants twenty rods, and they don't even want ten rods. Lots of people want about five rods, which is quite ample.

Phil Faucheux

Wivenhoe Horticultural Show

The Wivenhoe big event I remember was the Horticultural Show, which was held on what is now the King George V playing field, and I can remember that being held there [when it was still] a part of the Wivenhoe Manor Estate, which had been sold off. I believe there had been a Horticultural Association prior to 1914 as well but it had lapsed, but then it had been started again. That was always a big do. I can remember having the display stand there with the soldiers with horses, before the Army was really mechanised.

Don Smith

Our first show was 1965 in the Loveless Hall. But after that we decided to get bigger so old Claude Watsham came in handy, he said, 'Well, use the field,' so we put the show on at the back of the field there, behind Cross Farm, and that was quite a big show. That was the year of the World Cup, 1966, so we got another big marquee and you'd have thought you was at Wembley! All the cheering going on there – we had a big television screen what the local chap Mr Mason supplied us with, he had a shop here then. Everybody crowded in. We were a bit dangerous actually, we never realised how dangerous, because Claude put a lot of straw bales down to sit on and lots of the chaps were smoking so we could have blown ourselves up!

Phil Faucheux

SAS drop into the Wivenhoe Show

Major Tom Burt, being an SAS major, he got in touch with Hereford with the SAS boys, and they said, 'We'll come and do a parachute drop for you.' So they used to come each year, until the trouble broke out in Northern Ireland and then we lost that as well. But the SAS boys, they dropped three times for us and that was quite a spectacular thing in those days, parachute drops. And we had tug-o-war for the different villages and pubs, a pony gymkhana, a car gymkhana, all sorts of side shows, bowling for the pig and coconut shy. It was a big job. When I finished one show I had to work ahead for the next one the following year.

Phil Faucheux

Younger entrants

Years ago, when the show was held in tents up the ground, there was a lot more entries because we had more classes and there was anything up to about eight to nine hundred entries, where now, this year, we were up by seventy-odd entries. We had just under five hundred this year, including the children. This year it was slightly different because a lot of the younger people have taken on allotments, a lot of them showed.

Peter and Diane Duffield

Fellowship

I've always loved it. I still go in [to the allotment shop] every Sunday morning. They all know me, and I know them, and we have a laugh and a joke. And you talk about the weather, and when the hell's it going to get warmer, so we can put our seeds in! That'll be the conversation on Sunday. And lots of people have joined, who don't know so much about gardening, and you get asked a lot of questions. 'What should I do, Phil?' And as far as I can, I try to advise them. I'm a vegetable man – I give a lot of my stuff away, I have more than I want. I give lots to the old ladies. It's a happy life. I shall be in there Sunday, and lots of lads come in, and it's fellowship, isn't it?

Phil Faucheux

seven

Childhood and
Family Lives

*Farmworker and girl.
(Annabel Gooch)*

Infancy

Jane was four lbs and she was bottom first. Jane didn't put on weight and they kept her away two months in the Maternity Home and I had to express my milk every day and send it in. And Eastern National used to charge me sixpence. Used to put it on the bus in the morning and their gardener cycled down to the bus park six o'clock in the morning and pick it up. And I fed my Jane the whole two months she was in there. Matron wanted me to stay in the Maternity Home the whole time. And I said, 'Matron, I can't.' She said, 'Mrs Baker, that's your fifth child. Don't mean to tell me you don't need a rest!' I said, 'I never said that, Matron. How could I leave my husband at home at Christmas with four children and no mum?' I couldn't! So I came home on my birthday, the 18th December, and I'll never forget it! I came in the front door – Derek brought me home in a taxi – and they'd got a table here and they'd got a lovely birthday cake that they'd made for me, 'Welcome home, Mummy.' Now, how could I have stayed in?

Eunice Baker

Tasks for Boys and Girls

Granny's jug of ale

My Granny, who lived in Falcon Yard, there were three cottages there, I used to call there at twelve o'clock when I came out of school and she used to send me to the Falcon to get a jug of ale, which was about tuppence, and that's what she'd have at her lunchtime. And in the winter she'd let me poker it to warm it up! Used to stick the poker in the fire and stick it in! Ashes and all! And I used to go and get her bread and very often I used to buy a Coburg loaf. A round loaf with four knobs on top. And one of the knobs would come off in my hand so I'd eat it, and she'd think the mice had been at it!

Joyce Blackwood

Little fairy

Aunt Alice worked for Mr Heath. He was well known as an old tartar! But she always got on all right with him. And he was a churchwarden. My granny was always doing needlework and she used to make aprons for Aunt Alice. She used to have to have calico ones to do the rough work in, and all the frilly bits for the afternoon. And she'd made two new aprons and she said to me, 'Now, you're to take these round to Aunt Alice,' she said, 'You go in the back gate and up the steps.'

So I went and took these, and Aunt Alice said, 'Oh, come in. Thank you for bringing them.' An enormous man – he looked huge to me – came out into the kitchen and said, 'Hello,' he said, 'Have we got a little fairy in our kitchen?' Aunt Alice said, 'Well, that's my niece.' So he said, 'What's your name?' So I told him. There was a big dish of fruit on the table there, and he said, 'Do you think you could manage to eat this nice pear?' I said, 'Oh yes, thank you, Mr Heath.' So he looked, he said 'Well, she ain't no bigger than six penn'orth of ha'pennies, is she!' But he was well known to be a real old taskmaster, and all the children used to be scared of him.

But I went home and Granny said, 'Where did you get that pear?' I said, 'Mr Heath give it...' She said, 'What did you say?' I said, 'Mr Heath gave it to me.' She said, 'Good heavens!'

Freda Annis

Scrubbing for pocket money

No sweets came into our house for years. And when things did get a little better I had a 'Saturday penny' and I had to scrub the kitchen floor for that. And my sister cut the lawn with shears. No mower! And I can remember that I never had anything new. Well, neither did my sister. What she had was cut down again for me.

Marjorie Goldstraw

Taking lunch to the pit

My father was Harold Green and he went fishing. After 1935, he went to work for Loveless's sandpit. When I was about seven I used to ride a little fairy cycle, with a little basket on the front, and my mother would put his hot dinner in the basket and I would cycle over to him in my lunch break from school. And we used to then see what he was up to and I used to know most of the people at the pit.

Alan Green

Play Places

It was a totally different place, 2,000 or so people, when I was a child. It was a very safe place for children playing in the woods and whatever! We used to wander off for hours and hours and parents wouldn't worry, and we'd play around on the river – a totally different place. No traffic, not that many cars around.

I don't think our parents knew everything that we got up to, but we used to play in an under-ground World War Two air raid shelter in Rectory Road. That was our den, which was all fully kitted out by our gang, which was about a dozen of us.

Graham Wadley

Harvesting

We were lucky in them days, that was pre-myxomatosis days, and we used to go rabbiting in the harvest fields, with a stick. You couldn't afford luxury meals, the rabbits were quite good fare for all the local folk. I went with a stick, a walking stick, or a stick out the hedge, didn't shoot them! They cut the corn and you used to charge along behind the binder.

Brian Green

Watercress

We used to be able to walk down Spring Lane and across – there were streams all over there – and there was one stream had watercress in. The man

Demonstration demanding children's playground before opening of King George V Playing Fields, 1935. (John Stewart)

that used to live at the farm at the bottom of Spring Lane, he said to us one day, 'Do you want some watercress? If you come across here, I'll show you where to get some.' So we did. He said, 'You can cut through here and you can go through,' and we did. It was a Sunday afternoon and after we'd been to Bible class. So we goes home with a handful of watercress each! And it was nice watercress too.

Freda Annis

Elephants by rail

Where they built the Mulberry Harbour during the War, which obviously was the marshland between Wivenhoe Shipyard and Rowhedge, where there was a tollgate they used to have a yearly circus. I can remember, as a young boy, there was a circus there, maybe '36, '37, when they had elephants and the elephants in those days came by train and were unloaded and walked down to the circus.

Peter Sainty

The Pits

Bobbit's [Hole – the Pits] – we spent a lovely lot of time there, picnicking. And there was a garden with apple trees and a brook, and the brook was lovely, we used to paddle in it and we used to catch frogs and put them in our mugs and then let them hop. Leslie [my cousin, who grew up next door] was saying only this year how the policeman went after him once for sliding down granddad's haystack, because granddad complained to the police and he didn't know it was his own grandchildren doing it!

Hilda Barrell

What we called the 'Pits,' which is now all Dene Park Estate, that was the Pits, and we used to sledge over there in the winter if we had snow. I think courting couples – not that I knew anything about that then – used to use it in the summer time. But we used to go birds nesting over there, play Cowboys and Indians. It was marvellous.

Rodney Bowes

Our territory was the Pits, where is now the Dene Park Estate, which was a worked out sand and gravel pit, and it was grassy, gorse bushes, blackberry thickets, lots of rabbits. Wonderful for hide and seek and other wild games, and blackberrying in the summer. Further on towards Alresford, the Villa Woods, or Cockaynes Grove, we used to go there in the spring picking wild flowers – primroses and wood anemones, bluebells...

Sue Kerr

The Youth Centre

Kids now, what I've seen of it, they sit outside the Co-op. I used to love the Youth Centre. I thought that was fantastic that we could go down there and play ping-pong, or trampolining, or play darts, watch telly. But when my children were going it seemed to be vandalised one week and then it would be shut for a fortnight, and I just couldn't believe that. They didn't appreciate what was there – somewhere to go in the evenings if they didn't want to sit at home or they hadn't got homework to do. It weren't everybody, but I just didn't understand it.

Rodney Bowes

The Low Way

When we were little, one of the things that we used to do as a treat on a Sunday evening was to walk up to what we called the 'Low Way' – which is where the traffic lights are now – and watch the traffic coming back from the seaside. And that was a treat. And you'd call at the Flag for a glass of lemonade on the way back! But entertainment and those sort of things you did on a budget, you didn't go out and spend a lot of money or anything, you had to think of things to do that were different but cheap.

Joyce Blackwood

Tanks in the Broomie

Where we used to go to play cowboys and Indians, that style of thing, was what we called 'The Broomie,' which is where Broomgrove School is built. A lot of our childhood was Second World War and we used to play over there. But we had to be very careful because the early stages of the War they had the Second Royal Tank Regiment up there, and they used to come over the Broomie in the tanks for practice. So you had to just be very careful that you weren't hiding in gorse bushes as Cowboys and Indians or whatever you were playing when the tanks were coming around!

Tony Forsgate

No-go areas

There were one or two parts of Wivenhoe that we weren't supposed to go to – I think we did anyway! One of the areas was the alley near the Folly, going to the Shipyard. That was one of the areas where we weren't really supposed to play. And the other place that was forbidden purely for danger reasons, was the pits. We weren't supposed to go there because of being drowned and being caught up in the weeds, but we invariably did do that!

Halcyon Palmer

Selling acorns

There was always gangs of boys roaming around, doing what gangs of boys do – climbing trees, and we used to all collect acorns in sandbags and sell them over in Rowhedge for about 4d. a bag. In the summer months we'd collect blackberries and sell them over Rowhedge, they went for dye for uniforms during the War. It was a good way of earning a bit of pocket money. We used to collect hips and haws, too, to make the jelly and stuff for children. The worst thing about it, we had to pay to go over on the ferry. If the tide was very low we could walk across but that wasn't very often!

Glendower Jackson

Girls' play

Girls were honorary boys really. They weren't really girls. The real girls, you didn't really have anything much to do with. I mean, the girls who lived in Station Road who were with brothers, they just joined in everything up until the age of about eleven or twelve. Some of my best friends were girls who lived in the village, they were honorary boys. I mean, we allowed them to be boys for the time being! But they joined in and that was usually Cowboys and Indians round the wood in the playing fields. And the great thing was you had to capture the girls, which was always amazingly simple!

Dennis Sparling

We never had no bikes those days, we didn't even know what a bike was. We just rode on old pieces of wood or something like that. We had a skipping rope and we used to skip a lot. And then we used to make holes up the road where the school was and play marbles, on the ground, throw the marbles in the holes and that, but never to have any lovely games like the children have now. No, nothing. We used to have to go to bed at six o'clock. Have our tea and up to bed you have to go.

Ivy Knappett

Soapbox trolleys

Most children had soapbox trolleys. And Wivenhoe's absolutely perfect for a soapbox trolley. Derbys were held. You'd start at the Foresters' Hall, about the highest place where the road starts to level out. You'd get in your trolley, give it a good push, you steel your feet in a piece of rope, you can go right the way down the High Street to the Quay and if you weren't careful you'd go straight off the Quay into the river! It was great fun! You'd go well over half a mile without having to run, push or shove!

Pram wheels were a premium in those days because you want a good big wheel! Anybody had an old pram, 'Can we have the wheels, please?' I painted mine bright red! You couldn't buy paint, of course, this is all sort of paints that you found in your father's sheds. And if you asked for it he said, 'No,' you'd then still pinch some of it!

Glendower Jackson

Riverside Play

We played on the Quay. That was our playground. We had nowhere else to play. And where the Sailing Club is now, we always used to play on that bit. We always called it 'the Green,' and there was the bank down which everybody rolled down as long as you didn't go too far into the ditch! I fell in a time or two, I've gone over the Quay and I had a very nice cousin who pushed me over once! I never could swim. I never could swim. But, just lads, they were always on the Quay, up to their necks in mud and water and boats. My brother and them, they used to go off to where the *Rosabelle* laid, the boats down there, they had jetties out there, the boys used to dive off there.

Freda Annis

The *Cap Pilar*

On the river the *Cap Pilar,* this three-masted barquentine which had circumnavigated the world and came back to Wivenhoe to die, was moored just about where the Sailing Club is now, a little further downstream, and that was a great game. We used to go on board this old hulk, and the contents, to begin with, were pretty well intact. There were elegant chairs in the saloon, and gilt, with crimson velvet upholstery, which floated as the tide rose up and filled the hulk, and then they all sank down again. And gradually all disintegrated. But we used to pinch bits off that just for the fun of it! The belaying pins and any little bits and pieces that we could remove, we did! But that was very dangerous, playing on an old hulk.

Sue Kerr

Rowing for women

In the summer, we had a lovely time – we used to go on the river, when the tide was right, take our lunch and go up Mill Creek, or up to the Hythe. My granddad kept a nice lightweight boat for us, varnished, with lightweight oars – just for us. My auntie used to row, and I used to row. And one day, I went down the river with another aunt, and we took our tea with us, down to the 'Third Stile' – that's near the wood there – and a lot of porpoise came up under the boat!

Hilda Barrell

Swimming

I weren't allowed to swim in the river but I did! My mother caught me. When I was four and a half I'd swum across the river and I was half way back when she come down on the Quay because somebody had been and told her. I didn't realise that my father had lost a sister and it was red rag to a bull. We all swam across the river! For years! Even in the War.

Alan Green

I learnt to swim in the dyke beside the old pillbox. There used to be tons of kids down there. But my father used to threaten me about the dangers of that river. 'Very dangerous river. You're soon out your depth. And a strong current.' He drilled the fear of that into me many times. But many a time swimming costume and a towel have gone out the bathroom window and then I've gone round and picked it up! The boys were all going swimming.

John Bowes

Making makeshift boats

Everybody spent most of their time on the river. In the later part of the War, you could go to Colchester dump, down at Hythe, and buy, for 2/6d., an extra fuel tank that came off the aeroplanes. They were aluminium tanks which they would jettison when

Above:*Barquentine* Cap Pilar, *after her world voyage, 1938. (Glendower Jackson)*

Right: *Mudlarks on Second Beach, 1970s: from left, Leslie Meadows, Colin and Peter Smith. (Don Smith)*

they were empty. You would buy two, bring them home, cut a square in the top, bolt the two together, so you had, like, two tanks side by side, and they wouldn't turn over. And broom handles for masts, and an old sheet for a sail, and daubs of all sorts of colours of paint on these things. And all the kids, we had races.

Glendower Jackson

Model boats

I was never bored. I didn't know the meaning of the word. We always found something to do. We used to spend a lot of time making model boats, sailing them down by the riverside. I went to one of the local builders down there and got a piece of wood about a couple of feet long, and carved it in the shape of a boat, and with the help of my mother we made some sails out of a little bit of linen. It was something practical that you could do, you could enjoy with other lads. We were sailing races, in miniature, because when the tide came in, in those days the water used to flood over onto the marshes there and there were big like drainage ditches, although we used to call them 'fleets,' and they were probably about three or four feet wide, and they were just ideal for us to sail our boats in! In winter time, of course, we spent more of our time indoors but there again we had hobbies, model-making and all that sort of thing – aeroplanes. Anything we could make with a bit of wood or whatever.

Gilbert Whaley

Sticklebacks

We used to go fishing down in the marshes. We're talking about fish three inches long – sticklebacks! And kids used to go down with their nets and their jam jars and go fishing. On the land side of the wall there was a big drainage ditch and they were in there. And then, to get down to the wall we used to go through [part of the shipyard], where there was a big piece of concrete. That was our cricket pitch.

Alan Green

The White House

When we went down to the White House [just before Alresford Creek] for a day there were several families, and you'd have a packet of sandwiches and about a pennyworth of lemonade powder in a bottle of water and you'd go off down to the White House and you'd paddle around there. We didn't go in the water, not to swim. Some of the boys used to but none of the girls did. But I can remember paddling around there in all little rills and that, where the water came in when the tide came up and we'd be down there as happy as larks!

There had been a house called the 'White House' down there, it was across the railway line but there were apple trees still in the garden and part of the house was there. Well, one family in Anglesea Road,

Alresford Bridge. (Don Smith)

her grandmother had got a big iron kettle, and she used to bring this kettle and a newspaper and some matches, and there was an old fireplace left in this house and there was a well there so you could get some water and fill your kettle, and we used to collect up all the driftwood and light a fire. I wonder we didn't burn. They used to make this smoky old tea, in a blue enamelled teapot she had!

Freda Annis

Diving off the bridge

We'd go down with the tide, to Alresford Creek, and tie up in the Creek, go cockling, and getting these little winkles, in sandbags, and we'd come back on the tide. Swimming was lovely. We'd jump off the iron bridge at Alresford Creek, and, of course, the bridge keeper would chase us, and we'd let him get a few yards from us, and just leap off the bridge into the river! Yes!

Glendower Jackson

Winter Play

One massive slide

Wivenhoe High Street was one massive huge slide because there was no vehicles – only for doctors' vehicles – there was no other vehicle in Wivenhoe other than military, and the whole High Street, past the Greyhound, past the Post Office, down to the school, was one massive slide. And the old folk used to grumble at us for making this huge slide – and I can see why now!

Peter Green

It was called Bobbit's Hole. It's a housing estate now. Well opposite Bowes Farm the ground goes right the way down to the brook and that was magnificent when the snow was about. Everybody in Wivenhoe made a sledge, and to make the runners on the bottom you went down to Mr Worsp's canning factory – which is the Tiptree Jam people now – and all the fish boxes were bound up with an inch wide steel band. And the old boxes, he'd say, 'Help yourself,' and you would take all these off and take them home, polish them up with a bit of sandpaper, flatten them out, and you would nail them on to the sides of the runners of your sledge. And, of course, once you started, they would shine up and you'd go like mad!

Glendower Jackson

One girl, well, she was quite old, she was a woman really! Her father was the plumber and he made her this tremendous sledge which took five of us, fully grown lot on this, and we used to go down Brook Hill, Queen's Road, it wasn't made up. It had a gully in the middle where all the water run down. And we went to the top in Anglesea Road, all get on, and down we used to go and shoot up nearly half way up the other hill!

Freda Annis

Mischief and Discipline

Nobody did anything stupid, nobody stole things or broke things, that just wasn't done. There was no vandalism. If anything happened everybody knew who'd done it anyway, so you didn't get away with anything.

Dennis Sparling

The boys used to play tricks but I don't think they were vicious. I know one that some of the boys did. The men used to have watches in their pockets so some of the boys got an old watch and they tied it on a string. They got in the churchyard, they laid it in the road, and some old boy comes along and sees it and picks it up, gets it in his pocket, and they pulled it out! And another trick was with a bundle of wood. And old dears walking home with a bundle of wood, and that would suddenly vanish!

Freda Annis

Apple scrumping

I can remember scrumping apples at the bottom of Queen's Road. They had a nice apple tree near the pumping station that overhung the roadway, and they had a high wall and if you got up on the wall you could pick the apples! And my cousin was doing this one day and a special constable, Sid Ham, came along. And he came round the corner and caught us red-handed! Oh! I give him the apples that I'd got in my hand but he didn't see the ones that my cousin had got in his shirt! We got away with a few!

Alan Green

Fireworks

During the War you couldn't buy fireworks and I made some fireworks out of some cartridges. There was a crowd of us boys and I put one under Tilf Glozier's letter box – Tilf Glozier was our local hairdresser – and this went off and not only that, it broke the letterbox and the knocker which they had in those days. Eventually Sid Ham, our local constabulary policeman, called at my parents' house and I was confronted and I said, 'Yes, I did this.' I had to renew the letterbox, and I had to go and paint the door and Tilf Glozier, at the end of the job, gave me a packet of Woodbines!

Charles Scofield

All the boys did mischief. Putting fireworks in people's doors. Round by Clifton Terrace we'd stretch a string across and when Tolly Day the policeman went along we'd knock his helmet off with this string across and we'd run like mad! But I think he took it all in good part.

Glendower Jackson

String tricks

As teenagers we used to tie the knockers together. The first three houses in Alma Street, on the left as you go up, we used to tie their knockers together and just knock on one and as they opened the door they knocked on the others! And the best part of it was, when we used to do it on the first one, knock on theirs, and as they opened the door we used to run up the alleyway, on to their dustbin, and straight over the wall into the churchyard! We were dears! Little angels!

Alan Green

There were in those days hardly any motor cars in Wivenhoe and we used to put the string across the road and bits and pieces on the end, and catch a car! And one day I happened to let that slip out at home, laughing about it, and I really was in trouble for that!

Don Smith

A hell of a spark

You'd have hoops – you'd get a bicycle wheel, take the spokes out, and knock that along with a stick along the road. I got caught once, that was when I first started work, hitting a hoop along Belle Vue Road, and this hoop fell down so I picked it up and chucked it up and hit the electric light wires! Made a hell of a spark, that did! And never thought no more about it. The next day – because I was working for Ernie Cracknell on a baker's round – and I was in Belle Vue Road coming out of Mrs Curtis's, and as I come out her front gate, 'Whoa! Whoa!' that was Hasler, the policeman! A pair of black gloves went across my head, he says, 'That's for last night!' He'd seen me.

Charles Tayler

Cart before the horse

There was a family who lived in Station Road by the name of Curtis. There was four boys and a girl and they were a great family. And there was also

Children playing by the ferry shelter, c.1920. (Don Smith)

a chappie in Wivenhoe who was running a small greengrocer's round, and he used to have this little pony, and he was in Station Road one day and he stopped at a house – whether he was having a cup of tea or something – he was there some considerable time. And when he come out what the boys had done, they'd taken the pony out the trap, turned it round, so it then faced the produce on the barrow, and this thing was eating!

Don Smith

Throwing stones

I did end up in court once. At Wivenhoe they had a paddle-steamer called the *Pyefleet*, which belonged to Colchester Corporation. It was the boat that they did the oyster fishing with and it used to tie up near the shipyard, where the barrier is now. A couple of my friends they swam out to it and got on board. I didn't have any swimsuit but I was throwing stones at it and I broke the windows! And about three days later the police were round my house and I had to go to juvenile court. I got fined 7/6d. My father nearly killed me over that!

Glendower Jackson

Pledger the policeman

We had old Pledger! He was a real fat policeman type. Mr Pledger lived in Park Road and if the boys saw him coming they disappeared. 'Look out! Here comes old Pledger!' And the police had leather gloves in those days and he would always carry them in his hand – he'd just give them a clip round the ear. 'Now then, what are you up to?' And he would tell the kids off but the kids respected him. They knew they daren't play up with him.

Freda Annis

Home discipline

I've had the belt took off and had the strap several times! That done you good in them days. Now you can't hit them. One time I lost the paper money. I used to have to walk up to Alresford Post Office, I used to have to walk up for the newspapers on a Sunday, they used to be tuppence, and *News of the World* – penny a paper, they were. And playing about I lost the tuppence. So I hid in a ditch all day and they had to come and find me! I was frightened to go home! I knew I'd get the belt!

Charles Tayler

My father was a small man, he was shorter than me. If one of us started to laugh at the meal table, and once you start you can't stop, and he had very big thick hands for a little man, and I sat next to him and he used to clomp round my ear with this big hand and I couldn't hear any more until about

Marjorie Goldstraw aged three, playing at White House, 1920s. (Marjorie Goldstraw)

teatime. So strict. And when you went to visit relatives you didn't move about, you sat on chairs, and you don't get up or interrupt the conversation. And we weren't allowed to mix at all with other children, only at school, and not allowed to go to Sunday School because there were dirty things written in the hymn books! And how my mother knew that I don't know!

Marjorie Goldstraw

Youth: From the Lido to Courting

The Lido was, pre-1939, our local cinema, which was quite a laugh! The children, school age, there would be probably about thirty of us. You'd go there on a Saturday afternoon. You'd stand outside waiting for it to open. I can remember all the kids always wanting to push against these French doors, to open up. And it was always breaking down. I remember an appeal from the manager one afternoon, 'Would you please ask your mum and father to come along next week because we've got this film coming!' Originally, that building was built for the Foresters' organisation, and then became the cinema, and it closed just before the War. And then it was used for Welcome Home dances.

Don Smith

Chopper Hatch used to be also the projectionist in the Lido cinema. Because I knew him I used to every Saturday morning go and stoke the fire up with coke, to heat the cinema up, and I got two free tickets. And I'd sweep the cinema out. When word got around that I was getting free tickets I acquired so many friends who wanted the extra ticket to get in with! The first film I ever saw there was called the *Four Men in Grey*. But I did see films like *The Hunchback of Notre Dame*. They were great films! Everybody went. It was only Saturdays. I'd swagger in in front of the queue with my two buckshee tickets! Take a friend with me!

Glendower Jackson

Courting

At the dance in Colchester I said to my friend, 'There's a nice-looking chap over there.' She said, 'Yes, I was looking at him.' I said, 'Come on, let's go and sit by him. I bet he takes me up to dance before he takes you.' So I sat by him. Of course, he turned round and asked me to dance and that was it! And he met me the next day and we went to Clacton for the day. And he moved to Wivenhoe and stayed with us, the double bedroom in the front, and I had the little bedroom at the back. And David was a baker by trade. So he gets up in the morning to make a cup of tea. Brings the tea up. My father said, 'Where are you going?' 'I'm making Sylvia...' 'You don't step in that bedroom.' He said, 'You knock on the door and you leave it on the step.' So David never forgot it! He didn't get into my bedroom that morning, I can assure you! That was funny! [I met him in] August '58, and we married in November '58. I only knew him twelve weeks.

Sylvia Weatherall

In the Wider Family

Grannies and extended families

I lived with my grandmother for a long while because my mother only had two bedrooms and I had two brothers. So my grandmother really brought me up. And she used to live in the Alms-houses at Wivenhoe. My grandma made a fuss of me, didn't she! Because she was all on her own, and we slept together. She used to say, 'Come on. Cuddle up,' and she'd put her arms around me and we used to go to sleep in the same bed. Oh, that was really lovely. Of course I wasn't very old, about twelve years.

Ivy Knappett

It was always a great sense of community. Families, in my younger school days, hadn't dispersed, and so there were grannies, aunties – most people had extended families all around Wivenhoe, who would

Council houses, c. 1950. (Glendower Jackson)

all intermarry, so a lot of people were related! And everybody knew everybody's family history – good and bad, and misdemeanours and otherwise! But it was, as it is now, a very friendly and supportive community. Very safe. My mother never, even into her old age, locked her doors.

Sue Kerr

Housekeeping and Marriage

The front room

It was holy of holies [in my childhood], the front room. There was only a fire put in that on high days and holidays. The only time that settee was sat on was when my granny died and we had a bed down in that room till she died and the night nurse used to come in and sit on that settee! My mother could only afford three dining chairs to match, and it was beautifully done – lovely blue uncut moquette.

Marjorie Goldstraw

Buckingham Palace

[After we married] we lived at one time at 46 High Street. And there was no toilet, had to share with the next door neighbour. I'd no back yard at all to get the pram round or hang any linen. I had to walk round to Mrs Millie Gladden's, who lived at No. 1 East Street, to peg a bit of washing out – napkins – because it was all terry napkins then. And I had an old wringer screwed on the kitchen table, with rubber rollers.

Eventually I got a council house and I thought it was Buckingham Palace. There were two toilets there – one upstairs and one down.

Marjorie Goldstraw

When we first moved in here a councillor used to come round once a month to see that your house was all right. You didn't get a council house if you hadn't got children. The conductors on the bus used to call us 'Incubator Avenue.' Well, the Greens down there had eleven. The Welch's over there had seven. I've got six. Next door but one, Senior's had got six, and Mrs Dadds had got five. The Coats's had got five. Olivers had got five or six.

Eunice Baker

Woman's work

The women were drudges in the house, they wouldn't have time to go out. There was no modern washing machines or anything, it was all done by hand. There was a routine. Monday was washing. Tuesday was mangling because those big old wooden rollers, you could put it through and it flattened them, you didn't need to iron them. Wednesday was bedrooms. Thursday window cleaning. And Friday pull the house inside out to make it nice for the weekend. And always a Sunday roast. However poor you were, people managed, that'd be the highlight of the week. Midday. They were all clock-watchers. My mother – she always had the dinner served at 12 o'clock.

My housekeeping money never had to come to more than thirty shillings. And Family Allowance came in and I got nothing for the first child and five shillings for Stephanie, and I used to save that up for the shoes. I made nearly everything. I'd got a little hand machine, a Singer, an old thing. The lady next to the bakery, her parents – she was a spoilt only child – and they'd bought her this sewing machine and she'd never used it. Hand machine. And she sold me that for ten shillings. I made everything and I even knitted their vests and socks. And I knitted my husband's socks. He liked hand-made socks. When Stephanie went to the High School I made the High School uniform.

Freda Annis

Always knitting

My mother didn't go out. They were always busy at home. Her and Aunt Alice, in particular, they were always knitting and needlework. They made all their clothes. Aunt Alice's pet thing was knitting socks. I had the most elaborate lace socks she

used to knit me! And they never used to go out to anything, apart from going to church.

Freda Annis

Getting water

When my grandmother died my mother and father moved in to Border House. They moved in with my grandfather to look after him. At Border House we never had no electric, never had no sewerage. There was no bathroom. Used to have a bath on a Friday night where all the family bathed. Had a big well in the garden and my mother often used to say, 'Oh, get me a bucket of water, boy!' And she used to pull this water up out of this well, in a bucket, on a rope. Fancy my mother doing all that!

Charles Tayler

My mother and them used to have to go and get the water. You can go down two or three steps alongside what was the Fire Station there and that was what they called the brook, and they had to go down there and get buckets of water before they went to school or when they came home from school, for the mothers to use. That was drinking water. Yet I don't remember anybody getting any germs! And the stream runs right through Elmstead.

Freda Annis

A little bit simple

Granny had four sisters and there was one – and we were always told to be kind to her and she wasn't quite like other people, was how my mother put it to me. She was a little bit simple. I should imagine she was what they called a mongol in those days. But even then, a single sister had taught her to do needlework. She used to cut pieces out of pillowcases and things, get her to sew them for handkerchiefs and dusters, and she was taught to do vegetables. And her job on a Saturday morning

– I can see her now, sitting beside the dresser – was always to clean the knives with bathbrick [powdered brick], and she used to clean the forks with whitening and water mixed together.

Freda Annis

Very much Wivenhoe

Mother was one of a large family and she was a good parent. My grandmother had relations in London, and my aunt went up there and went into service for one of them. And all her life, that one, she was more modern than the other sisters. My mother was still very much Wivenhoe and so was her younger sister. But my other one, Aunt Letty who went to London, she was the belle of the ball type! Her whole lifestyle was different. More broad-minded. Her social life was much more going out, enjoying herself, dances, all things like that!

Don Smith

They expected it

One of my aunts she married a Scotsman during the First World War so, of course, she went up to Scotland to live and it was quite a long time before they came home. And she came home one Christmas and we were all there, and my uncle said, 'Was there any mustard?' So Granny said, 'Ida, get him the mustard.' So Ida looked, she said, 'Oh no, I don't, mother. He's got two arms and two legs and if he doesn't know where to find that now, in this house, it's about time he did.' She said, 'You always made us wait on the boys, and I hated it. They never had to wash up.' And she said, 'We always did, and I'm not waiting on him!'

Freda Annis

Wartime splits and peacetime reunions

In 1950 my parents' marriage broke up. We were away on holiday, Dad and I. Mum didn't want to come and when we came back she'd gone. So I didn't see her for thirteen years – from the age of thirteen till I was married, with my son. I was very upset. At thirteen you want to tell your mum everything. You can't tell your dad private things so everything had to be kept to myself which is awful. But Dad was very good, I will say that. He wasn't one that would preach sex or anything like that, but he was good in his way. But it was hard.

She wrote just out of the blue when I was married and said could she come and see us? She had regrets, I think. But she'd fell on her feet because she was in Hyde Park one day, and sat down for a rest – she'd been working in a hotel – and a lady sat beside her and mum got talking to her and she said, 'I work for a Member of Parliament in Guildford,' in a place called West Clandon, and she said, 'I'm retiring.' So mum said, 'Oh, I wouldn't mind that job.' She said, 'Well, I'll have a word with the boss when I got back' – millionaire. He had big restaurants in London and he used to go all over the world. So he rang the hotel where mum was and he said, 'I'll come and pick you up tomorrow and bring you over to West Clandon and interview you.' He sent a limousine there and back for her. Mum got on so well with him he said, 'Can you start tomorrow?' She said, 'Yes.' And she was Sir William Stewart's housekeeper for eighteen years.

The first meeting with mum was very difficult because I looked at dad's side and I thought, 'He had it hard, really.' To come home in 1945 and mum was pregnant with – it was not his child, obviously. How very hard for him to open the door and find your wife eight months pregnant. And I think mum thought, 'Well, I'll have it and have it adopted.' She didn't think dad was going to come home in '44, she thought he'd come home in '45. But of course, he was home when the baby was born and there was rows. It was hell really. You can imagine what he was calling the baby. And mum said, 'Well, I'll have her legally adopted,' so she put her up for adoption. [The baby's] father was a Czechoslovakian soldier. Just one of those things, wasn't it?

Sylvia Weatherall

Many years later, with the help of internet professional searchers, Sylvia was able to rediscover her lost sister. They had an emotional meeting and since then have kept in touch.

Laying abed

When we got married we lived in a house on the Quay. New Year's time and we had a double bed there and we had a window half way down, open, so you know how daft we must have been at that time! That New Year's, half way open, the window! And they would call out, 'Cheerio, mate! Happy New Year!' 'Happy New Year to you, Dick,' you know, 'Happy New Year to you, Rob,' and all things like that. And we used to keep a-down, and one was going that way down, like, to Clacton way, and the other one was coming up the Colchester way, up the Hythe way, so they met just here and they'd say, 'Happy New Year, mate!' And we kept the window right down so we could hear them, you know! 'Same to you, Fred, mate. Happy New Year,' and we laid there with the window half open and that must have been ever so cold! And we wasn't cold. No, we just laid and listened to them and we thought how lovely that all was laying abed, and the moon was a-shining, and lovely stars, then. 'Goodnight' to them as they passed each other by the ferry.

Ivy Knappett

eight

New People

Martin Newell. (Dennis Marsden)

As a maritime village, Wivenhoe has always been in contact with the wider world, and for centuries, people have been moving in and moving out of the village. But in the last fifty years the growth of new housing and sharp rise in population numbers, the development of an artistic community and the arrival of the University of Essex, have brought particularly important changes to Wivenhoe's social life.

Coming to Wivenhoe

Green roots

The family originates from Harwich, and my grandfather was 'Friday Green,' as he was nicknamed, because he would never start his working week on a Friday. If he hadn't been to sea all the week, then he certainly didn't go on a Friday, because he would feel he was starting his working week on a Friday! Grandfather was apprenticed to a Captain Carter, and he used to sail in the Americas Cup – yachts of years ago, as crew – and he sailed into Wivenhoe, at a very early age, apprenticed to Captain Carter, and this is where he settled.

We go back a long way in the days of sail and fishing in Harwich, which in those days was quite an important fishing port. They used to fish Iceland from Harwich, under sail. Quite an epic journey in itself, just to get there, let alone fish and then come home with the catch. Quite incredible! Cod fishing, in those days, was very prolific.

But that's where we originate from. And it's strange, because one of my ancestors actually married an Icelandic woman. Because, if you were up off Iceland, and you were into bad weather, then, it's any port in a storm, and things happened from then on I suppose. So, yes, we've got an Icelandic connection as well.

Ken Green

Friday Green. (Don Smith)

French master canner

I was born in Sandwich in Kent, where they play golf. My grandfather came over from France, he was a master canner because the French people were canning everything long before we ever did. And in 1901 he built a small factory at Deal. Father moved to Colchester because they were catching herring and sprats in this area and he was interested in canning these as well. They called them 'brisling,' the sprats. And the pea industry was coming alive in Essex so they canned peas and all sorts of fruit. Of course, the whole thing went bankrupt because nobody would eat out of a tin in England – it wasn't till the Second World War that we all started eating out of tins. And then he had a factory in the Hythe. And dad lodged at the Shipwrights' Arms in Wivenhoe. So I followed father when I was one-year-old, in 1924.

Phil Faucheux

By bicycle from Lancashire

I was born up in Blackburn in Lancashire, and spent the first ten years of my life up there. 1930, we came down here because at the time there was no work up in the North. My father was a plumber. Together with probably thousands of others my father came down here to find work. Fortunately he had somewhere to go, inasmuch as he was in the First World War and he was stationed in Colchester, met my mother during that time, they married, and so he was able to come down and stay with my grandparents in Colchester to find work. Came down here on a bicycle! Gradually he found a little cottage down in Brook Street and I came down with my middle brother with the furniture in the van! I came with it! And that was the start of my life in Wivenhoe.

Gilbert Whaley

Prisoners of war

I was aware that at least two German prisoners-of-war worked on local farms, and married local girls and stayed on in England after the War. But there was really no animosity towards these young men that worked on the farms.

Sue Kerr

Risking the War blockade

Wivenhoe was shut off because of the War, but we risked it, and we cycled over. So then we were rather taken aback. For £450. It was called the 'Store House,' because lots of yachtsmen stored their gear in the room at the back, and was in an awful condition. The stairs had been taken down, so that Dr Radcliffe could build his Wivenhoe One-Design. Well, we didn't move down until February 1945 because it wasn't ready, and we weren't supposed to come here. Dennis used to come down, but I was too scaredy-cat, in case we should be arrested – again, because we were a couple of men, and I was out of the Army for being queer, and he was a conscientious objector,

one hardly really liked to put one's head above the parapet!

Richard Chopping

Irish platers

We got that order so quick, we hadn't got anybody to do it, so the manager went to Belfast, in Ireland, and got a whole load of Irishmen over here, and where the old Falcon used to be, that's where most of them lived. Oh, there were some characters there! Oh dear! They liked their drink! They were Irish! They were good tradesmen. Some of them finished up their time over here in Cooks's.

Charles Sansom

The Geordies

When the Geordies were there, they went to the pub dinner time, and they went to the pub on the way home, then they went to the Brewer's Arms, and the Black Buoy – the nearest pubs to Cooks's, so you virtually fall out of Cooks's and into the Brewer's Arms!

John Bines

Painting murals

When I came to Wivenhoe in 1954, the first thing I did, once I came off the station, I went into the Grosvenor for a pint! And there were two lads in there, painting a mural, and I learned, later, it was the Dan brothers, Phil and John, and they did this job for nothing, except they did it for the beer money! Yes! They thoroughly enjoyed it too, I'm sure!

Frank Hodgson

We wanted to stay

When we came in 1974 we very quickly decided this is where we wanted to be, and to stay, and we really didn't have any intention of going back up North. We liked the house. We liked the schools, we liked the friends that we made very quickly.

We began joining clubs and societies. I joined the Sailing Club, and found it very welcoming. Jan [my wife] became more involved in the Gilbert and Sullivan, and the Scouts and Guides Association, and the school's parents' association.

Alan Tyne

Because of the sailing

I came to Wivenhoe in 1975, because of the sailing. My husband was a film sound recordist who went on location a lot, in any year he was probably away for three or four months of the year, and we used to live in Ealing near the film studios. We'd got a boat, and once I'd got the two children it seemed to be this terrible labour gathering everybody up, potties and nappies, and driving off to Rochester, where we kept our boat, it was just a nightmare! So we decided, why don't we move to where we can keep the boat and commute to work? We'd sailed here once before, and we saw the advertisement for Wivenhoe in the paper, and we remembered this wonderful place, so we moved here. But then when we came here, there was so much else going on that we hadn't even suspected, it was fantastic!

Janet Turner

The disenfranchised

I was overcome by Wivenhoe. It's a very very special place, isn't it? It's got the *joie de vivre*, it's got the life, it's a bit small-time if you're in a bad mood, but it's got something. It's partly it does attract a lot of eccentrics and artists, and it's got the University. I've always got on with people that are disenfranchised, one way or another. They don't think they're eccentric, but they're the best ones. You can communicate with them.

Guy Taplin

Grass around it!

As we drove in 1985, we passed Millfields School, and looked at the vista down the River Colne.

And I couldn't think of a better place to bring the children up. Millfields – physically, it's got greenery, it's got grass around it! The school that my daughter went to in London, was just a concrete jungle in Seven Kings. And the teachers seemed to have time. They knew all the children, they knew all the parents. There was great interaction. We would see them at different functions in the village, and it really was a community spirit, and it's exactly what I was after when we were moving out of London.

David Craze

We liked the look of it

We looked at businesses throughout East Anglia, we went up to Norwich and Bungay and all sorts of places. We saw this one in Wivenhoe, liked the look of it, it was within our price range, so we came down to Wivenhoe, saw the people here, made an offer, a little bit of haggling, and we eventually agreed on a price, and decided we would move to Wivenhoe and take a little Post Office here. This was October 1985. So that's how we got to where we are at the moment. I've got three brothers, two of them had Post Offices as well, so I was the third one! And I became a third-generation sub-postmaster because my granddad, my dad, and then me! Something I swore I would never do! But having gotten into it, glad it happened! Fabulous! Immediately we were made very welcome and we thought, 'Well, this could be the right place for us,' and it was!

David Burrows

Incredibly friendly

I'd lived in different parts of London for about thirty years and '85 I left, actually, in a very distraught state, for various reasons. I wanted somewhere small, where you didn't have to have a car before you could start walking.

I found Wivenhoe incredibly friendly. I'd never known a place like this. I ordered some York stone to pave in the garden. I waited for ages and ages, and one day, I was looking out of that window, and

I saw an absolutely enormous lorry, that had come along this lane. It was incredibly big, and it had got jammed, couldn't go backwards or forwards, and in the middle of all this enormous lorry, was this tiny, tiny little bit of York stone. So I went out in real trepidation, because I'd come from London, and I was sure people were going to come out because the road was completely blocked, nobody could go one way or the other, and they were going to descend on us and beat us up, I was quite sure. But instead all the cottage doors opened and people came out bearing trays with mugs of tea and plates with sandwiches! And they all settled down to have a street party! I was absolutely dumbfounded!

When I went shopping, it was up a hill, and it wasn't that I was carrying anything heavy, but I was trudging uphill, and a car stopped beside me, and said, 'Get in, and I'll run you to the top.' And he just took me to the top of the hill and let me out. Things like that. And when I moved here, I deliberately kept that little wall very low, so that people could see the garden, and people used to stop and discuss the garden. It was a lovely garden then, it had hollyhocks and foxgloves. And the people who stopped, they started to put things on my doorstep, for me to plant in my garden – plants that they'd dug up from theirs, they had plenty of them growing there, and they brought me ones over, and people who were growing things on the allotments, used to put lettuces on my doorstep.

But what was much more extraordinary was that they used to hug me, complete strangers, because I didn't know anybody yet, they used to give me tremendous hugs in the High Street. I was bewildered! And somebody said to me, 'Well, it's because when people come from London, generally they put up high walls and a big gate, and they shut off from us. You've done just the opposite, you've invited us in, and we can never thank you too much.' And it was quite extraordinary! There is an amazing feeling of friendliness in Wivenhoe, that still exists there. I find it an astonishing place.

Leila Berg

Writers and Artists

Wivenhoe has been a centre for artists since the 1940s. From the 1960s many academic writers from the university have come. Other writers whose voices are in this book include children's story-writer Leila Berg, and Wivenhoe-born novelist Olive Whaley, writing as Elizabeth Jeffrey, whose Cassie Jordan *is a story of the nineteenth-century village. Wivenhoe also has its poet.*

Village Poet

I started making a living as a proper writer some time about fifteen years ago. Now, in late middle-age I'm thinking, I'm not a celebrity, I don't want to be. A certain measure of fame is useful, because if somebody wants a bespoke poem written, then that is what I do. They say, 'Could you write us a poem for such and such?' And that's a good position for me to be in. But where do I fit into Wivenhoe? I can go into the local pub and busk. And if they want a poem written about the cycle path I can do that. If Andrea wants a poem written for her wedding, I can do that. I probably wouldn't get paid what the *Indy* pays me, but I'll get a drink out of it. I just work on a sliding scale. I can tell jokes. And I can do a spot of gardening. So I can be useful.

At least I wear interesting clothes on the way to the newsagents! People have given up asking me why I'm at the newsagents at 8.30 in the morning, with a dusting of eye make-up and teddy boy's jacket and a strange hat on and a brightly coloured shirt – I don't think it costs too much to make an extra effort and it annoys the androids and amuses some of the people. I feel very much that I'm a part of the social tapestry in Wivenhoe. I should just get an Arts Council grant for just walking around looking interesting!

Martin Newell

The First Artists

Richard Chopping and Dennis Wirth-Miller were the first artists to settle in the village.

When we came to live in Wivenhoe in 1944, we vowed we wouldn't mix with the village at all, socially. Because we wanted to work hard and get somewhere with our paintings. But we led a very naughty life, because we were spending money that we hadn't got, and were getting to get a bit free and easy, sexually.

Richard Chopping

Freudian or Jungian?

Well then Margery Dean, and Dr Dean, they were rabid Socialists, wished to get to know us, because we were painters. So Margery put a card through the door, everything crossed out and written in, 'Are you Freudian or Jungian?' 'We have tea at about five o'clock, every Tuesday and Thursday, and do call.' Eventually we did.

Richard Chopping

Francis Bacon

We had Francis Bacon in the Station Hotel, and Richard Chopping and Dennis Wirth-Miller. I had the situation, one day, where they were all drunk, I eventually chucked Dennis out, and Francis said he wanted to go back to London, so I escorted him over to the station, put him on the train, chucked all his baggages in behind him, and Fay said to me later, 'I hope you made sure all the baggages went aboard,' she said, 'there was a painting in every one of those!' I'd just chucked a few million quid on to the train!

I always found him quite charming. He was very good to us, wasn't he? But a face that, oh, told a thousand stories. There seemed to be a lot of agony in his face. Quite frightening in some ways. And I think Dennis was professionally jealous of Francis, because Francis is one of those few who really achieved fame in his own lifetime. One of the more amusing days was going up to the Arts Club when Dennis had just thrown bricks through most of the glass paintings and God knows what else, because Bacon had told him he wasn't much of an artist, or something like that!

Colin Andrews

I don't think people bothered

I've never really regarded it as a Bohemian place, but I don't think anybody here has ever given homosexuality a damn! I think, because of the seafaring chaps, they probably were more sophisticated. I don't think anyone minded. Wivenhoe people, by and large, are jolly nice. It might have been considered a bit rum, two men, not in the Army, one of them half-German and a Conchie, they must have thought it a bit funny, but I don't think people were bothered, I honestly don't. I don't know that we had a hard time at all. No, we didn't.

Richard Chopping

I think the reaction of Wivenhoe to gayness has always been very positive since I've been here – which is thirty years – and I think that's just got easier and easier. I've ever had one incident in my entire time in Wivenhoe, of being called a 'queer'. What goes on behind my back may be another matter. But that's my experience. So it's a very easy environment for gay people to live in. That's contrary to all the books, which say, 'Escape to the city where you'll be safe. Don't stay in a village'. There's not a big gay community here as such, but I am saying that quite a number live here, and quite easily.

Ken Plummer

Francis Bacon was great friends with Dickie and Dennis, but they were always at each others' throats – terrible battles and fights, and screamings,

Richard Chopping and Dennis Wirth-Miller, c. 1995. (Dennis Marsden)

came here, they got talking to a lot of the old boys on the Quay, and they got used to them. Dickie Chopping, coming from Fingringhoe Mill, he was a bit more accepted as near enough local. But they didn't take very much to the arty crafty type. Oh no, they were very much against that. But I think, eventually, they tolerated them.

Freda Annis

Gail Cross and Pam and John Dan

Eventually, there came Gail Cross and her husband, and Gail Cross's brother-in-law, and his wife, who had a pub opposite the old Fire Station. Gail Cross painted, her husband painted, and was Art Master at a school. Very Socialist. A big chip on their shoulders, because they weren't at all well-off, and they thought of us as snobs, I'm afraid. We tried to be friendly and have them to dinner and it didn't work at all.

Pam Dan came as a girl, with her mother and father, and they lived almost next door to the Greyhound. John Dan built a pottery there and made his pots, and Pam painted. So then you have a nucleus of Pam and John, and Gail and her husband.

Richard Chopping

and drunken brawlings, and rows, and bitter sulks. Dickie and Dennis have had lots of metropolitan figures of fame, infamous or famous coming down, so they were another tributary of fashionable London life of that period, who came down to visit them, coming to add to the gaiety of the village.

Sir Peregrine Worsthorne

They want to do a day's work

They thought they were – artists, good Lord! 'They want to do a day's work' was the attitude! The only people, and I think they were criticised, were Dickie Chopping and his pal there. When they

I came from West Indies to Wivenhoe in 1954/5, and ended up marrying John, many years later. We rented a house on the quayside, and I used to do a lot of work down by the sea wall – of reeds and rushes, and cows in fields.

Pam Dan

John Dan was very local. His mother was one of the schoolteachers. She used to play the piano very well. If ever you went to something in the village there, Etta would be playing the piano. And John became an extremely talented potter.

Halcyon Palmer

Art in the Brewery Tavern

Pat and Jack Cross moved into a little cottage opposite the Brewery Tavern, and then they sold that to buy themselves into the Brewery Tavern pub. Jack Cross was a very good painter, he was more of an intellectual painter and they started up an art type pub, but it was for everybody – the shipyard workers, when the shipyard was doing well, they used to come and drink in there. The art people used to come, and the Brewery Tavern developed into a small art gallery, people's paintings on the walls.

Pam Dan and Louis Footring

All the artists' paintings were on the walls in the Brewery Tavern, and really, the artists' activities then, were at its height. And if there was an overflow in the pub, we just used to move into Jack's front room, and take over that, and carry on drinking in the armchairs!

Bill Heslop

The art people

Shortly after they took it over, Jack's brother, Roy Cross, and his then girlfriend, Gail Cross, came down from London, and bought a house on Anchor Hill. Roy had been a prize student, at the college in Liverpool, and was an up and coming painter, an expressionist painter. Before that, another painter from London, Tony Young with his wife, also came to live here. And then hot-foot from Cornwall, Mike Heard, he was with the Cornish painters. And another sculptor came, Ted Atkinson, who was Head of Sculpture at Coventry School of Art time. He was also from Liverpool. All this happened very quickly. The artists, I suppose about thirty of us, were very close-knit friends, and we saw each other a lot. It was like one huge family.

Pam Dan and Louis Footring

Roy Cross did some wonderful abstracts of the local landscape around Wivenhoe. It reminded me of Ivan Hitchins, in the same use of slabs of colour. The other very popular artist was Mike Heard, and he pursued his individual, almost Turneresque way,

Mike Heard in the Station Hotel. (Colin Andrews)

Members of the Arts Club. (Tony Young)

painting the light effects down by the sea wall. His bread and butter pieces were his excellent coloured drawings. He was a very fine draughtsman.

Bill Heslop

people have gone to her classes at the Sailing Club. She encourages and sees the positives in any scribble or daub her pupils make.

Annie Bielecka

Peter Lang and Pam Dan

Peter Lang was a very good local artist. He'd been deputy town clerk of Lowestoft, and then Town Clerk of Wivenhoe. He painted local scenes and the herring women who followed the fleet from the North of Scotland through the thirties and forties, down the East Coast. He was married to Pauline, who was a healer, and they were both very caring people, keen on the environment. After retirement, Peter was active in the Wivenhoe Society for many years.

And of course we have Pam Dan. She's a wonderful painter and a very gifted teacher. Many

Ernie Turner, Wivenhoe's Primitive

Ernie was born in Wivenhoe in 1899. His uncle was Albert Turner, Captain of *Britannia* in 1920-30s, and his three brothers all were related to the sea. Ernie's early years were to do with yachting. He worked in the Wivenhoe Shipyard during the War and after as a shipwright, then moved to Cook's shipyard and retired in 1964. It's thought he then took up painting, though he had previously built model yachts. He started off with watercolour, moved into oils, then used household paint or anything he could get hold of, painting on hardboard, cardboard, the sides of cardboard boxes and began to sell them. In 1964 the Wivenhoe art community had started to flourish and Pam and John Dan were intrigued by his work. Pam bought a couple of his paintings and he became in great demand, churning them out. Nearly all his work is of local scenes, Wivenhoe Quay, Fingringhoe shore, Alresford Creek, mainly smacks or barges sailing on the river. They are naïve or primitive in that there is little sense of perspective , no sense of depth, Lowry-like figures. His earlier paintings are considered to be his better ones. Ernie just painted what he saw.

Richard Barnard

The Arts Club

Founding the Club

It was 1966 that the Arts Club was formed. George Gale, he was a journalist, a Fleet Street man, he came here to buy a house, and he bought a huge house, Ballast Quay House, with lots of land and a stable. Big stable, it was a courtyard, with the stables. George used to come and drink in the Brewery Tavern, and so was impressed with all the painters arriving, and their work put up on display on the walls of the tavern, which was a very basic pub, floorboards. It was very good, terrific atmosphere.

Pam Dan

George Gale used to go and have a drink in the Brewery Tavern on his way back from London. Chatting and talking in the pub, they had the idea that they'd have this Arts Club in what were their cow byres and stables, and the idea was that Roy Cross's brother and his wife would run it, would live there and run the bar and mount the exhibitions.

Halcyon Palmer

So George Gale turned these outhouses into the Wivenhoe Arts Club. Cleaned up and painted up and it was a beautiful job. It comprised of a very

big gallery space, beautiful gallery, which led you into a very big bar space, with tables, wooden tables and chairs.

It pulled in a lot of artists from out of Wivenhoe as well, a lot of interesting people – there were poets, there were writers, artists, drama people. They brought Fleet Street with them as well, because they were their weekend guests in the big house. George, being a well-up journalist, knew Ted Heath, and invited him down. He was leader of the opposition at that time, invited him down to open this Art Club.

Pam Dan and Louis Footring

George Gale was a larger than life figure, with a gruff voice, and had been a great star journalist on the *Guardian* – very very clever, a great friend of Kingsley Amis. He had, by then, moved to the *Daily Express*. And Pat, his wife, was a very colourful, larger than life personality too, loved social life, and they bought this very large house in Wivenhoe, at Ballast Quay, looking over the estuary. And they filled it, at the weekends, with all the Kingsley Amis crowd, and a lot of Conservative and Labour politicians, lots of writers and artists. And George Gale was on an early radio phone-in programme, and people would come and stay and if they wanted to get hold of George, they would ring up him on this programme, 'Where did you steal my toothpaste?' So lots of people came, and there were lots of parties, and it turned Wivenhoe a bit into a celebrity spot: Wivenhoe was appearing in the gossip columns.

Sir Peregrine Worsthorne

Arts Club activities

We had some wonderful shows. All the Wivenhoe artists had exhibitions there, fairly frequently. We had very interesting project exhibitions. We had one called 'The Nude,' and a lot of artists not only in Wivenhoe, but outside Wivenhoe, took part in this. We had drawings, sculptures, we made films for it, poetry, and it was just absolutely amazing, and attracted hundreds of people.

It was a membership Club, but it was rather open to be invited. Lunchtimes, in those days, lots of pubs closed on Sundays, but we were open Saturday, Sunday, it was most evenings.

The Arts Club did wonderful yearly Arts Reviews. Little pastiches, there was generally a main play, written by Jack, and this would be sending up various people and happenings of the year. He was a good writer. George himself was a good pianist. On November 5th, we had a wonderful fireworks display, for the whole village to come to, and there was hot soup, and foods to be bought and eaten, and half the village used to go up there.

William Dean's Hog Roast! Every New Year's Day. It took him twenty-four hours to cook it. He was our local doctor, he was still practising, and he absolutely got his chef's cap on, and his big apron, and was turning this thing and basting it, and I think it went on for about twenty-four hours, this big cooking, didn't it?

Pam Dan and Louis Footring

The Arts Club and the village

I think the village was quite sympathetic, in the end, to us. To begin with, they were a bit suspicious. There were a number of people from the University then, they were attracted to that sort of atmosphere, because you could always go up to the Arts Club and find somebody to talk to, on any subject you liked! The local doctors partook, Ted Palmer, and William Dean. And then, George Gale's wife's sister – Jackie Claiborne – who'd married an American man, he was the Assistant Attorney General in the States. And they bought a big house – Wrawby House, in Park Road – and then they became involved as well, and they brought their friends. So the whole thing was very exciting. You had lawyers, you had architects, you had painters, sculptors, poets – we had poetry evenings, didn't we, poetry readings.

Pam Dan and Louis Footring

I think, anyone of my age, most probably has quite some good memories of Wivenhoe Arts Club. It was a club for all kinds of people. They always used to hold dances at the Arts Club, and they used it as a gallery as well, so it was all good fun.

Tony Allcock

What sort of impact did the Arts Club have on Wivenhoe?

Horror! There were some very good ideas, and we had some very good people, nice interesting exhibitions. But there were stories of wild parties, some of which were exaggerated, I have to say! But after all, this was quite a conservative (with a small c) little place, and you hear these wild stories, and if you've lived in a little place like this all your life, that it must have been quite shocking to quite a lot of the older people. But we had a lot of fun as well, and it did bring a breath of life to a rather stuffy little village.

Halcyon Palmer

1984: The Demise of the Club

When George Gale moved from Wivenhoe, sold up, the purchasers of the club area, and the cottage at the end, said they wanted to keep the club. But then they decided that they were going to make some money out of it, turn it into habitation. And then began a long battle to get us out, with all sorts of underhand dealings and awkwardness, like trying to block off the courtyard area so that we couldn't park there. Once at a ball that we had, they crawled along the loft from their part, and they drilled some holes through the wood pine ceiling, and dropped stinkbombs down through the holes! Into the club!

We had some sort of tenure, but effectively, it didn't work. And we did discuss with the Co-op, Mike Heard and myself conducted some discussions with the chief executive of the Co-op, and he was okay about letting us have the downstairs rooms. But people had lost heart a bit, and didn't think it would fit in properly.

Louis Footring

The magic was broken by this time as well, the magic that kept it going all those years. It was just that George Gale and Pat left, and although we did try very hard to keep something going, it didn't gel.

Pam Dan

Since the Arts Club

I am optimistic about the future for art in Wivenhoe. Some local artists are internationally known, their work is highly regarded and widely exhibited. There's a wide variety of work made here, painters, quilters, photographers, sculptors, glasswork, textiles, potters. The art is made in sheds, studios, garages and spare rooms, and there are classes and groups working together. I feel fortunate to be living here, surrounded by other artists, many of us working on our own. If you're stuck with a piece of work, there's always somebody you can go and talk to.

Annie Bielecka

Art and the landscape

My own textile land and seascapes are inspired by the wide skies of East Anglian, and the river and sea have inspired other artists too. For example, Guy Taplin lives in a house that's like a museum, much of it maritime art. He collects the most incredible stuff, mostly made of wood. He's got things hanging from the beams everywhere. We had a little beach house next to him and his family, and we used to collect driftwood. Guy makes his birds from driftwood. That's a special place where he can go, completely on his own, and get away from Wivenhoe, to be with the birds and the wildlife.

Annie Bielecka

Driftwood sculpture

My work is accessible to everyone, I very much hesitate to call it art, but it doesn't really matter what you call it. I think birds have always appealed to me, and I've always been interested in folk art and primitive work – self-taught artists, and black people in the southern end of America.

But the driftwood pieces were huge, well, sometimes you couldn't bring it back, it was as simple as that. I had a couple of rowing boats scattered about, and so you could get it on those, and get it to somewhere where you could get a car down. Or you'd tie it up. You usually find lots of rope around. You carry a knife, and you could tie it all up, and carry it on your back, and just lug it home. It's hard work, but worthwhile.

Now I go abroad a lot and get it. Portugal and Greece. There's a lot more wooden boats out there, a hell of a lot more, and their colours are very bright – blues, reds, maroons. They're breaking them up all the time, and they're left in sand dunes and marshes, and it's hot and salty, so all the wood gets bleached out, but that's just what I want.

The tools I use are more or less the same. A big bandsaw. A contour sander, come off of that, use a hand grinder into the bits you can't get into, and then I just finish off with rotary flexible drives, which are much smaller. It's all to do with curves, and you reduce it down to what you want, as quickly as possible really.

Guy Taplin

Rough tools

Guy Taplin was a great help in those days – still is – but especially then. We were talking about making things, and I decided I was going to make a big fish. There was a lot of driftwood in those days, tons of it, very plentiful. It was a material I hadn't really taken much notice of before. I made this big fish, and I think Guy bought it off me, so that set me off on a journey!

I was very inspired by the materials, and I liked poking around up the river banks and finding

Sculpture by Max Tannahill. (Dennis Marsden)

these things. Some of them were huge pieces, like big logs. I used to bring them on my bicycle, unbelievable loads! Used to have a big stack of it outside the shed. I like the old wrecked boats, the old clinker-built boats, they're very good for mounts, putting stuff on them. But they're getting really quite rare.

The very early stuff I did, I tried not to do too much with them, in regard to the shaping. But I realised I was going to have to work a thing, instead of relying on this serendipity, where you just find something that looks the right shape. So I got a few more tools. My tools were very crude. I only got a set of chisels recently. I was using saws and rasps, and hammers, quite rough. Very rough. Not a very scientific approach to the whole business, but I kind of liked that. I liked that Luddite thing. I found one of the tools, an old hammer, down on the shipyard. It looked like something somebody had made as an apprentice, when the shipyard was still operating.

Max Tannahill

The University

We didn't like it at all

We didn't like the University coming. I'm sorry, but we didn't like it at all! I was very very much against it. Well, they were looking for ground for the Hospital at the time and I still think that if Charlie Gooch had have waited and let them have that for the Hospital, it would have been a beautiful place for the Hospital. But we didn't like it – especially the older people. And in the early days we did get some rather weird characters. We really did. There was one fellow, it was nothing to meet him in pink satin breeches and boots and a great big feathered hat walking up the road, and a pink satin coat! Well, it was drugs, I think, a lot of it. But we've got used to it.

Freda Annis

The ploughman's sit-in

At the university they don't get into ructions like they used to. When they first got there they sort of had a sit-in, didn't they? And when we used to be hoeing sugar beet, you could hear the music at six o'clock in the morning, with their sit-in.

Brian Buckle

The troubled times

I think we all had mixed feelings about the University, really. We were excited to have it but I think we felt we were being sidelined rather than included. Some of us felt a bit resentful about that. For example the medical part of it all went, straightaway, to Colchester. I know my father felt it, that they were not even really consulted about it. But then, of course we had a lot of people who came, and then we had all that problem with people jumping out of windows, with the LSD and all that sort of thing.

Halcyon Palmer

I think that the student riots at Essex had a particularly sharp aspect, partly because the campus was so isolated. If what you wanted was clubbing and the bright lights it wasn't ideal, and Colchester was and is a small provincial town without many of those amenities. But it was accentuated by Albert Sloman's philosophy of having a small number of large departments concentrating on research rather than teaching, and the students – *some* students – undoubtedly felt neglected. And then, thirdly, there was the complicating factor, which is that Colchester is a garrison town and there was unrest in Northern Ireland and the military intelligence were very interested in what went on in the University. And then, of course, finally, it was close to London and close to Fleet Street, and with George Gale and Peregrine Worsthorne living on Anchor Hill, which meant that if you wanted a piece about rioting students then Essex was always bound to provide one. So those were the particular reasons, I think, why Essex suffered more than other places. So I watched in some horror and alarm. And then it quietened down a bit.

John Ashworth

Early doubts and new life

When the University first came here, that was when all the young angry brigade were in evidence, and a lot of them rented a house in Queen's Road and the goings-on there were quite shocking. We saw people falling out of windows, and the drug squad sitting outside waiting for them. But the coming of lots of new people to the village has certainly brought new life to it. We had a Dramatic Society but nothing like they've got these days with your Gilbert and Sullivan, and your pantomimes. No, that's all helped a lot.

Joyce Blackwood

The big change

It's changed. The big change was the University. The *big* change. I noticed that when I had the hairdressers. When the University came, and it was a very good thing, it opened Wivenhoe up. We were very insular. And, of course, it brought so many interesting people here.

Helen Douzier

Of course, the University has made a huge difference to Wivenhoe. It did it a good turn because it brought work, for one thing. So many people employed up there are from the village, aren't they?

Marjorie Goldstraw

University enriches infant school

When I was Headteacher at Broomgrove Infants School, what I liked very much about it was that, because of the University, we had children from all over the world. So we were able to ask them to talk to the other children about their own countries. And one term we had tables all the way round the hall and items were brought from various parts of the world and the children spoke about them, and their parents came – so the children learned a lot about different nationalities from their own friends.

A little Japanese girl used to greet me every morning with a bow. Lovely!

Hilda Taylor

Working at the University

Library work

I went in August 1970. I was in the towers first looking after the women, and then the job came up in the library. I was getting the books in the morning, at half past seven, that were left out by the students, and then putting them back on the right floors, which took till about nine. I was there 1974 to 1987. I liked reading. I would often get a book down and have a go, especially medical books, just to read and see if I can learn anything.

Sylvia Weatherall

Nice girls and boys

I went to work at the University in about '68. Just looking after the students in the Towers, cleaning their rooms, making their beds – which they don't do now – and generally looking after them. It was quite nice, there was about ten of us women in one tower. I stayed there until I was retired at sixty. The students were very kind. If they went abroad or anything, they'd bring you back a present. Yes, there were some nice girls and boys up there.

June Sansom

University electrician

I went in 1970. I'm a baker by trade and I was having trouble with shift work, and this job come up, I just went as a lamp changer. Then I gradually worked on all electrical jobs, like repairing the cookers and all the lighting, never become a qualified electrician but it paid well and it was quite good. They were very friendly. Everybody knew one another, all painters and cleaners, carpenters, plumbers, they all got on well together.

They used to have a University Christmas Party. Everybody wanted to go, didn't even work at the University! It was such a first-class do. Then we used to have football matches and darts matches. The students against the works staff. We got on quite good actually!

Dave Weatherall

Department secretary

There were hundreds of secretaries! You'd do the staff's correspondence and memos, take dictation, and then you'd maybe type a chapter, photocopying. I think things were much more relaxed then, and the ivory tower and the idyllic lifestyle was possibly fairly true. I can remember in the summer vacations playing ping-pong in the office. But I would think, from about the mid-1970s, that all rather changed, and there wasn't the money. When I started the University paid better than anybody else in the district.

We've had some lovely students over the years, really nice people. And very few nasty ones. I liked the more mature ones! Academics – some of them are great, but some of them aren't. I mean, put them in front of the photocopier and they've had it if something goes wrong!

Mary Girling

Professors at sea

Founding Professor of Biology at the University, John Ashworth went on to be Chief Scientist to the Cabinet Office in the 1970s, where he urged the future importance of climatic change and the radical social impact of new information technologies – and went on thinking about such questions while he also enjoyed sailing the Colne.

I was very interested in the possible radical effects of new communication technologies on a number of social as well as scientific areas, and wrote a couple of reports, and helped the BBC produce a *Horizon* programme, 'When The Chips Are Down.' In those days, the discussion tended to hinge around microprocessors and chips, and I was somewhat notorious because I produced chips and a valve – 'You see, that is a valve, and a chip,' and I showed that to Mr Callaghan's Cabinet, and said, 'What you have to understand is that a thousand of these valves are now on this chip, and that is going to revolutionise everything. This isn't just about electronics, it's about society and how we do things.' And I endlessly pressed this. I was thought to be mad. But, of course, it's all come about, even more radically and more quickly than I had anticipated.

And that was due in part to my sailing. One of my sailing colleagues when I'd been at the University of Essex, who was in the Department of Electrical Engineering, was a nice Swiss man, Guy de la Fontaine, and he, off Clacton, when we were becalmed and anchored, so we had to anchor otherwise the tide would have taken us, he explained to me – off Clacton, I shall always remember it – how these chips worked, and what dramatic things they might be able to do. And that was why I was so sensitised to the issue when I went into the Cabinet Office.

John Ashworth

nine

Narratives of Change: War, Local Politics and Struggles

Ellen Primm and her sister in their wartime overalls. (Ellen Primm, Marcel Glover)

Many of the changes which have so much altered Wivenhoe over the last fifty years have come about through the choices of individuals or small groups, rather than actions at a community level. Factories and shops have opened or closed down; people have moved into Wivenhoe or moved out; couples have chosen to marry or not, or to have more or fewer children – and all such decisions reshape the wider picture. But changes have also come from events at a community level. Some of these have entailed open struggles. The memories here begin with the fight against an outside enemy in the Second World War. With later peacetime conflicts, the focus shifts especially to local debate about the protection of Wivenhoe's environmental heritage.

1939-45: War

Schools and Evacuees

I started school here in 1942, and the very first day, September '42, we'd been there about half an hour, and the siren went, and we all filed across the play-ground, into the shelter, and I can remember the headmistress, Miss Smith, saying, 'Come on! Come on! They can't wait for you!' Because there were some aircraft having a dogfight over the river here. Anyway, we got in the shelter. But, of course, these old shelters, they were just cement seats to sit on, and very damp and dark. When we came out, she suggested to us that we got our parents, or mum, to make us up a little cushion to sit on, a little pad, because in the cloakrooms there, we all had our own pegs. And the next day, my mother had made me a little pad, but one of my young friends there, Ken Mullins, he came in with a damned great pink cushion, and I remember her saying, 'Oi! You can't have that,' she says, 'that takes up three spaces'!

Ray Hall

Lackadaisical teaching

The school, of course, suffered quite badly because the teachers who were of useful age obviously went away to war. So they recalled teachers who had taught at the school and had retired, and Mrs Dan was one of our teachers. She was a dear lady who came back, I suppose probably in her fifties. She seemed like 150 to us kids but she was a dear sweet lady. So we had a fairly lackadaisical teaching at school because half the time you were at school, you were in the air raid shelter anyway!

Dennis Sparling

Everybody took an evacuee

When the War broke out, I always remember, we had all these women and evacuees come down from London. And everybody took an evacuee, but my father wouldn't. He refused point blank. But some of the women came as well. Oh, it was awful. And they pinched the women's husbands! Oh, dreadful goings on! And they, a lot of them were dirty and flea-ridden. A lot were from round the docks.

Marjorie Goldstraw

Suddenly, in 1940, we had hundreds of kids dumped on the village, these very strange people from London. They couldn't understand us and we couldn't understand them. They had a most peculiar accent and they thought we spoke a foreign language! But they came, and were billeted all over the village. We had a mother and two children in the pub. They were East Enders, they lived in a too dense area. We were poor but they were even poorer.

The impact of the evacuees on the school was that one week you went to school in the mornings, the next week you went to school in the after-noons. And sometimes you had combined lessons for things like sports and so forth, but in the main the two sets of children were kept separate. And so we only got half-time schooling – that's why I can't spell!

Dennis Sparling

War Bride

When men were going abroad and were wanting to marry you could go to the MO and sort out a problem. And I came home on leave on the Monday and married on the Thursday. And I went up to London and got everything – lovely dress and everything – on the Tuesday. You couldn't book up anywhere. Even all the hotels in Clacton were closed, and the beaches were all barb-wired, so we wouldn't have had time to book. So we did it at home. And the baker my mother had her bread off, he heard all about it and he said, 'I've got baking a wedding cake for a GI, for a Yank,' he said, 'I'll take a little bit of this and that out of the Yankee's cake, and the icing sugar as well' – because that was all rationed – 'and you can have two tiers.'

Marjorie Goldstraw

Bombers

We was all in darkness all the while. No lights in Wivenhoe at all. Nothing at all, because the planes going over, going to London. The Jerries was off to London, to bomb London, and so they used to go over and they were a frightening turn out.

Ivy Knappett

I lived on the Cross, and quite often we used to walk along the railway line and the river bank and walk up Spring Lane. It was about [September] 1942, when a German aircraft decided to have a go at one of the trains in the night – it bombed it but it missed it. They used to see the firebox reflection on the smoke, so they could dive into them. And the next day my father and I walked down there, there was five big craters in the corner of the field! Because they were going to plough all those fields in Broome Grove, Mr Gooch had to plough them, they weren't his ground, but he had to take it over during the War. My father worked on the farm at the time, for Mr Gooch. But he was about to plough that field, for the War effort, and he went down just to have a look to see if they could fill these craters in.

Ray Hall

A prize find

Standing in the garden you could see these dog fights going on high up in the sky and the vapour trails and the swirling planes, and as a child you're not aware of the implications of it all. It all looked just jolly good fun, as a spectacle to watch. And often, in the morning, there would be shrapnel, very jagged bits of metal, in the garden, which was a prize find. I had a collection of shrapnel!

Sue Kerr

Home Guard

William Loveless told me a good story. During the War Charles Gooch was the Captain of the Home Guard. Loveless was the sergeant, and he'd had military experience, he'd helped with the building of the Baghdad Railway. Anyway, somebody had given Gooch a sticky bomb to demonstrate. So they go out in the field up there and they put out one of these large metal trough, fodder things. There's a tin lid over and this great sticky thing on the end – a sort of little tin thing you opened up. Anyway, Charles Gooch got this thing and he said, 'Well, what you do is, you walk straight up to the tank, and you stick it on like that!' Just in time old Loveless grabbed him, dived for cover, told the whole lot of these chaps who were lined up to flatten themselves at once before the whole thing went off! And there was metal shards going in all directions and all hell broke loose! Fortunately nobody was hurt!

Dr Ted Palmer

SAS

Real crazy men

I can remember the regiments up at Wivenhoe Park. The first lot that were there were the Lancashire Fusiliers. The next lot were the Royal Fusiliers, and then the Tank Regiment. And the last lot were the SAS – Special Air Service. They were the maddest crowd ever, they were! The things they did! They used to come flying through Wivenhoe in eight or nine sitting on a Jeep, hanging out the side! They were real crazy men! That's why they were in that regiment, weren't they!

Glendower Jackson

Major Tom Burt

Tom Burt was the officer in charge of the SAS up there. He was a character. It's unbelievable, the bloody things he done, really! I mean, he wanted to make a path down his garden, and he couldn't get any concrete or asphalt, to make this path, so what he done was he took all the corned beef from up the big house, that was all in big tins, and laid all these tins down his path! That's true! That would be about 1942, I think, when they started the SAS.

Charles Sansom

The Wartime Shipyards

Whatever the cost

The government instructed the Rowhedge Ironworks, as a company, that they needed Wivenhoe Shipyard, because it had a dry dock, and that was the only dry dock available between Lowestoft and Tilbury. The place was six feet high and brambles, and there was rubbish all over the place, and so a lot of the riggers and labourers went over to clear the whole place up. It took a long time. And then the dry dock had to be pumped out. Fifteen feet of mud in it!

In 1942 I started work for Mr Crout, the chief draughtsman on drawings for wooden towing vessels, and by the time we started building them, they became the 105-foot motor minesweepers. Then I was told that I'd got to go over to Wivenhoe and open up the Drawing Office. So we went over there and we worked on these motor minesweepers until '45.

Robert Buckingham was in Wivenhoe Yard as the managing director. Before the War, his profession was cut glass. He was Chairman at Rowhedge, basically, because he was a shareholder. He was a very nice man, and he had a good team around him. It wasn't a commercial affair, it was run by the Admiralty. I never got involved in costs in those days. You got an order to do something, and you did it, and whatever the cost came out at, it was paid.

Bill Webb

Come and pick some trees

We had two Admiralty superintendents, and they lived in Wivenhoe. But nearly all of the people there were house builders, and they were then handling great oak frames. The planking was two and a half inches thick, the minimum. Bilges and strakes [side planks] were much thicker.

I've been out with Stephen Cranfield, the yard manager, we used to go to the country estates, as a jaunt really, 'Would you like to come and pick some trees today?' 'Yes, I would.' 'Well, we'll go to Thetford, then.' And, there were areas where these 300-year old oaks were growing, some were in historic parks, and I don't know who had the authorisation to cut them down, but that wasn't our worry! And we'd take some templates with us, and we'd size up these trees, 'That's a good one for planking,' might mark a dozen trees, and within a day or two they'd be cut down. When you think of the keels, and the stern posts and transoms, at least 250 trees went into each minesweeper – 250 trees! Now, we built nearly thirty of those – that's 7,000 trees!

Bill Webb

Women in the Shipyard

Ellen worked as a carpenter in the Shipyard from 1940-44.

We were making RAF uniforms at the beginning of the War. Then I left and went to the Shipyard, because I had to register — I was twenty, all girls of twenty and over had to register, so I had to register, and I said, 'Well, I don't want to go in the Forces.' That didn't appeal to me. I loved my home and my family, and I didn't want to go away! So I decided to go to the Shipyard, and my younger sister said, 'I'm going to leave and come to the Shipyard with you.' I worked in the Joiner's Shop, doing carpentry and joinery! And I thoroughly enjoyed every minute of it!

I never thought I'd ever work in a shipyard. We worked in the Joiners' Shop doing carpentry and joinery, and there was just four girls in there. There was a lot of girls in the Paint Shop, two women worked in the Store, one worked with electricians, and there was quite a few worked in the Boat Shop, because there was more boat builders than was the others, and so there was more girls worked in there. And we really enjoyed working there. It was lovely!

And do you know, the men were amazing. They were very good to us. Because we thought they'd resent us working there, but they didn't. They helped us a lot, they told us exactly what to do, and if we couldn't get a joint right, they'd help us out.

We were making parts for the boats. I specialised in that one. When you used to go in the boats, and you used to feel quite pleased, and you can think to yourself, 'Well, I did my bit during the War!'

I was sorry to leave. That was a wonderful experience after doing tailoring all those years! We went back to tailoring, after the War.

Ellen Primm

The White City

Mulberry Harbour sections

The White City, just in front of the railway station, and facing the marsh, was a huge white building, which was used for storage. But when the Whale Project came along, they took that over, and that was used in the dry, for laying out and marking all the plating for these things, because they were quite a size. I suppose they were forty feet square, if not more. We didn't know what all that was for.

Launch of minesweeper, 1942-3, blessing by rector, Rev Alan Gosney; White City on the right. (Don Smith)

The first thing we knew was people coming up to the office, obviously dignitaries from some War Department, and they had plans, but it was not spread around.

The next thing we knew was that material arrived into the Yard, and forty welders from various parts of the country were billeted around the town, and they stayed until the job was finished.. That was just before the Christmas, and the two were launched, and towed away by tugs, around about April. From the tollgate, almost to the ferry itself, is where [for their Project Shark for protecting the French waterways] Dorman Long set up their casing construction, and they had great scaffolding up the whole of the way along there, and it was really like a production line. They looked like a big flat box. And they were all towed away. But we had no idea. We had no idea at all. And you think that 6th June, the D-Day, and they reckon there was about 45,000 people [nationwide], don't they?

Bill Webb

Welcome Home Dances

The War was on when I had my children so my husband had to go to war, and I had Jennifer and I took her down to see him in the train, and he waved to me – and I didn't see him for five years. So Jennifer didn't see her dad not until she was five years old! She didn't even know she'd got a dad! And when he come home she looked at him as if – you know, 'Who is he?'

Ivy Knappett

During the War they had dances nearly every week, and it was wonderful! 'Welcome Home dances,' where you were raising money to welcome home the soldiers after the War. They was held at what was called 'The Lido' then, that used to be a cinema up the road there. You'd have a dance one week and a social the next week, which meant that as well as dancing you played games. Adults, not just

youngsters – anybody who wanted to go there. And of course the blackout was on, so you'd come home in pitch darkness.

Joyce Blackwood

Street parties

My parents used to run 'War Weapons Week' and 'Dig for Victory' week, and we used to have tugs of war and fancy dress parades on the playing field. When the War ended, we had street parties – the Falcon Yard was our bit, and the whole of Alma Street had big tables all the way down the middle, and I can remember we had jellies. In those days, we thought it was the height of sophistication!

Halcyon Palmer

1953 Floods

My father was a fireman – part-time – and we had a bell in the house. Well, on the night of the '53 flood, that was the 1st February, and I should think it was about half past twelve when the bell went. Well, when I got up in the morning, that was a Sunday morning, my mother said, 'Must be a big fire somewhere,' she said, 'Dad hasn't come home yet.'

So I rode round to the fire station, and there was a fireman there, Nelson Crosby, and I said, 'Where have they gone?' He said, 'The phones are dead.' He said, 'I don't know where they are.' He says, 'Bloody good tide last night.' And all the water was still in the Folly, and there was people sloshing out. It should have been low water, but that was still quite half up at least. I looked, and I said, 'That's some hell of a

The Brightlingsea branch line after the 1953 floods. (Don Smith)

High tide at the Quay.

tide,' so I rode round towards the railway station, and, sure enough, all over the marshes, and they were just getting old Mrs Woods out of the Tollgate House, out of the bedroom window, in a dinghy. It went into the dry dock, flooded the dry dock out. It was up in the Fitter's Shop, in the yard, it was up above the bench level. All in North Sea Canners, old Mr Worsp's, all them houses there were desperate. And it got the railway station.

Ray Hall

Wivenhoe Society
(Founded in 1966)

Margery Dean

[In the 1945 council election] my mother stood for our local Labour Party, and I think she was top of the poll. But she was a bit of a champagne Socialist. Somebody on the council suggested that [they should] knock all the houses on the Quay down, and put a row of council houses there. She had very strong ideas of what was aesthetic and what wasn't, nearly had apoplexy, and certainly completely put paid to that idea! [Later] it was mooted that somebody had bought the old ship-yard, and wanted to have wood importing, and to store wood down there, all over the marshes. And she just thought this was horrendous! And so in conjunction with George Gale, she had the idea of starting the Wivenhoe Society, to try to prevent this yard coming, or at least to contain what was done there. And also, retaining the nice things that we had in Wivenhoe, old buildings, which would be a great shame to destroy. So she was the secretary, and was really instrumental in banging on people's doors and saying, 'Won't you join?'

Halcyon Palmer

In those days there was a great division between indigenous Wivenhovians – those who had lived here for most or all of their lives – and the new-comers. And when the Wivenhoe Society came along, Councillor William Sparrow, who was land-lord of the Rose and Crown, was moved to ask, 'Who are these people who haven't been in the town five minutes, trying to tell us what to do?' But the newcomers were very much better equipped to see Wivenhoe in perspective.

Nicholas Butler

The membership has remained about the 300-odd level. But as in any organisation, the active mem-bership tends to be small – those who have the time. Thirty-odd years ago more than half of the committee were working people. Now more than half are retired. Generally, now, it's people who have lived here a long time and may not have been born here but perhaps, like me, who have been here 35 years or so, who may be incomers but have rolled their sleeves up, got their hands dirty, and to some extent been accepted as locals.

Austin Baines

When I first became a town councillor, there was this feeling, this animosity, almost, between the Wivenhoe Society and the Town Council. Having been chairman of the Wivenhoe Society for six years, when I became a town councillor I insisted that they had a representative, and that one of the town councillors would go along to the Wivenhoe Society meetings to take back their views directly. I think the animosity was political. It was thought of as the lefties, stirring things up and wanting all these things to happen. There was this mistrust.

David Craze

1970-73: Wivenhoe Woods

I was involved in the fight over the Wivenhoe Woods. I still have the photographs of them knock-ing the trees down, which we never actually used. The problem was when they sold off what used to be known as the 'goat field,' which is Beech Avenue really. A local builder was involved in part of it because I had some dealings with him over the thing but then they started edging further and further into the wood. This was partly the begin-ning of the Wivenhoe Society. We saved the woods, in the end. Some of it went, but not much.

Dr Ted Palmer

When I joined the Wivenhoe Society committee, Wivenhoe Wood had become an issue, particularly because of the developments which were going on, on land owned by Leslie Kemble, who owned the eastern spur of the wood, some of the northern parts – the development which is now Beech Avenue, Woodland Way, Parkwood Avenue. People were concerned that we should not lose any more of the woodland, and that we should to get public access to it. There was access to the southern end of the wood, and to the hawthorn section, because that belonged to the Urban District Council as part of the playing fields, but north of that, the wood was in private ownership.

So there was considerable agitation to prevent the wood from being further built over. Not, in fact, I think that very much of it was built on, it was the scrubby outsides. In the end the Urban District Council, negotiated, or served a Compulsory Purchase Order on the principal owner, just before they disappeared in 1974, Leslie Kemble having been voted off the Town Council in 1971. He had been a Town Councillor for some time, but he was not as popular with so many people as he had been, and he was voted off in favour of someone who had campaigned for the public acquisition of the wood. But there was a lot of correspondence, a lot of agitation in the newspaper. And this was focused by, and the bureaucratic stuff was done through the Wivenhoe Society.

Austin Baines

Kemble, the builder, wanted to build executive type houses in the woods here. And I said, 'Our children go down there for the bluebells and the chestnuts, and bird watching,' I said, 'No way are we going to let him build in there'. There was a fancy dress on the Sports Day, on the playing field, and I dressed my girl up all in ferns and leaves and branches, as the woods, 'Keep Out the Woods!' Teenage boys come up, 'Why do you want us to keep out the woods?' 'No dear, we want you to keep the woods. We don't want Mr. Kemble building in it, do we?' So they went and painted his gate that night! We kicked up havoc. Everybody in Wivenhoe, got them all on our side, 'We ain't gonna let him build in there. No way!' And we've still got our woods!

Eunice Baker

Having lived most of my life, from the age of four at the top of the village, and remembering all the farmland, and having seen all the estates being built,

[I know] we nearly lost Wivenhoe Woods. That was one of the good things that the protestors did do, because they managed to stop that.

Pat Alston

1971-75: The Falcon

The Falcon came slightly later but in the early seventies, when an application by the brewers to close the pub, demolish the building, and replace it with a little brick supermarket, probably even smaller than the present Co-Op – which did upset an awful lot of people. They didn't want to lose the pub, they didn't really want a supermarket down there, and they didn't like the way the brewery were doing it. And this was seen as an assault on the Conservation Area, and the principles behind the Conservation Area, replacing what was considered to be an eighteenth-century building, but was obviously older, with a not very pleasant mid-twentieth-century brick structure. Eventually that was resolved when the ministry listed the Falcon, and the applications were called in and, essentially, the brewery gave way. They did not get their planning consent.

Austin Baines

The Falcon. (Don Smith)

Wivenhoe UDC Council

Wivenhoe Urban District Council was formed in 1898, one of the smallest in the country, but eventually running a range of public services, including water, sewage and a fire station. In 1974 it was absorbed by Colchester Borough Council, and replaced by the Wivenhoe Town Council, which has fewer powers, and acts more as a pressure group within the Borough.

My dad was chairman of the Wivenhoe Council for many years, on and off. My dad was always Independent. He said, 'You don't need politics in a local thing like this.' No, when it was Council Meeting night, Dad used to say to me, 'Come on! Polish my buskins!' Because he used to wear leather buskins with his boots, and I used to sit on the doorstep and clean his buskins!

Betty Govan

Uncle Edwin was on the Wivenhoe Council with Bill Loveless and Percy Chaney, Billy Cracknell – and they were all tradesmen. In fact, in the twenties and thirties era, it was businessmen, completely, which ran Wivenhoe. It was non-political, there was no political persuasion. It was never anything other than the person they were voting for.

Peter Green

A lot of celebrities

A lot of celebrities sat on the council, really! There was Percy Chaney, he used to keep an ironmonger's shop. Edwin Green, who owned the fish shop, and Alf Bowes, the farmer. Mr Garnham, who was the farmer at Lower Lodge Farm, and Jack Canham was a builder. They were the ones that I remember early on. And then there was a woman – much to their disgust – got on the council, and she was Mrs Bessie Richardson. Her sister was a schoolteacher here. They came from a local family. And anyway, she was Labour and well, it just wasn't done! And there used to be some sparks fly! They used to report all these Council Meetings in detail in the paper, you see. And they got arguing. And she said

to Mr Bowes, 'You're no gentleman.' And he said, 'No. And you're no lady, or you wouldn't be here!' It must have been in the late 1920s.

Freda Annis

My grandfather was involved in local politics. I think, when Wivenhoe was an even smaller village, and the local farmer was on it, and the local builder was on it, I expect they were all corrupt as buggery, truth be known. They were there, I think, looking after each other.

Rodney Bowes

Set ways

The Wivenhoe Urban District Council consisted of old Wivenhovians, and they were very set in their ways indeed. There was Miss Grasby, a former schoolmistress, and Mr Chaney, an ironmonger, and William Sparrow and Mr Kemble, the builder. Far from running the town, they were rather run by the people who ran the big estates and came in. Leslie Kemble was voted off the council, to his considerable displeasure, and he didn't put up again. He was a builder and it would have been very lucrative to put more houses in Wivenhoe Wood.

They were succeeded by the Wivenhoe Town Council, whose powers are, on paper, much more limited, but felt themselves, as it were, in a dialectic, or even in conflict with the Borough Council in Colchester, and they were much more concerned to fight for Wivenhoe.

Nicholas Butler

Wivenhoe Town Council

The Town Council are the voice to the Borough. There are eleven people now. It got so busy, it's a fantastic amount of work. Not only have you got the full town council meeting once a month, you've got Planning, you've got all the other meetings, all the sub-groups, plus all the different

Demonstration against port expansion, early 1980s. (Dennis Marsden)

functions going on. And when you're mayor you put your life on hold for a year! But I wouldn't have it any other way, it was fantastic! Absolutely fantastic!

David Craze

Same hymn sheet

Politics never really been very significant on the Town Council. But without the political parties there wouldn't be a Town Council, because it's been the political parties that have persuaded people like myself. It was Betsy Grasby who put the idea into my mind, at a Scout and Guide AGM that she attended, she told me bluntly, 'You ought to be on the council,' I think were her exact words! And Topsy Jennings got to hear about this, and I got talked into standing for the Conservatives.

Peter Hill

People would say, 'Oh, there were famous rows between different people who obviously were at different ends of the spectrum.' But I just found that you couldn't pick out who here is Labour,

Conservative, Liberal or Independent. You couldn't, because they were all, ninety-five per cent of the time, they were all singing from the same hymn sheet, pulling in the same direction – basically, what is best for Wivenhoe.

David Craze

1984-5: The Port and the Miners Strike

The anti-feeling

The port had then been going several years. There was quite a lot of controversy, first because they fenced it all off. What was open ground, and people could walk across down to the river, and walk to the old ferry point, then became closed off, and they re-routed the footpath – or tried to – and I think the locals didn't like the fact that it became a wharf. But it created quite a bit of employment, and it had become established in use as a port, but purely for timber. When we moved in, of course we changed it to general cargo. I felt quite proud to be able to come back to my home town and be bringing some business. So I was quite saddened with the anti-feeling. I wasn't really ready — I wasn't really aware of the dislike that local people had for that.

Pat Alston

There was a picketing of the Port site at times, a lot of people down there protesting. Basically, they didn't want the amount of lorries coming down to the Port. The Port had been a wood yard, which was two or three lorries a week, and when the Watts brothers bought it, and developed it as a port, it became a constant stream of lorries, all day, every day, and people were concerned about the amount of stuff that was coming into the Port, and the fact that there was dust blowing off of the lorries. They had a lot of talc come in, and then the coal dust, and that blew off the lorries, into the roads, and then it rained, and it totally blocked all of the drains. So people were protesting.

Pat Smith

You may have already heard about the controversy that went around the cargoes that we handled, in terms of not just the noise and the intrusion of the lorries trundling up and down the village, but also the dust that came from the cargoes. There was an initial protest. We used to have frequent visits from environmental health, when locals complained. And there were at least three court appearances. The cases were brought by groups of local people. The Wivenhoe Society, I think, were quite strong instigators of the complaints. And any planning applications that went in were fought. We had to go to appeal on most of it.

Pat Alston

It was never enough

We tried at least twice, to negotiate with the local council people, landowners, to have a spur road put in, that would come through the University, and along the river, that we suggested, would bring Port only traffic, so that would take all of the lorries out from the main drag — which we would have paid for. It would have meant negotiating the release of land further along, But also to extend the wharf upstream, so we could then have guaranteed to have kept all the 'unsociable cargoes' further away from the housing.

In our attempts to keep it as clean as we could, we have, on several occasions, knowing that the cargoes would produce dust, and knowing the prevailing wind, which was actually westerly — towards the village — we've actually sent our ships across to Colchester Dock and paid for them to discharge the cargoes, and paid for them to be ferried around to be put into our store. We felt we worked really hard to try and contain it. But it was never enough. Never enough for the villagers. They were never satisfied. We've paid to have people's windows cleaned, we've paid to have people's cars cleaned. We felt that we tried extremely hard to appease the locals, but we always felt there was a particular group of people — headed up by the Wivenhoe Society — that was determined that they would never be satisfied with whatever we did.

Pat Alston

Dancing out the pile driver

They were extending the Port onto the marshes. And to do that, they had to bring down a great big machine, pile driver. And it was extraordinary. The pile driver came slowly down into the village and was just about to cross the bridge. And everybody just came out of their houses, and stood in the street, at the end of Station Road. We were singing and dancing and just stopping this pile driver from going down to the marshes. We did turn it back. But unfortunately it snuck down in the middle of the night about a week later.

Celia Hirst

Complicated verdict

The Port in the 1970s and early 1980s was a wood yard run by a company called Meredith's. It was then bought by a Colchester property developer, Danny Watts and his brother, David, became managing director of Wivenhoe Port Ltd. David started to bring in materials like soya and fish fertiliser and in the 1983/84 miners' strike, started bringing coal into Wivenhoe, and then ferried on heavy lorries up through the High Street. I was then on the Town Council, and there were four of us – Glyn Davies and I from the Town Council, Austin Baines – who was also Town Council, but Wivenhoe Society – and Len Horner, also Wivenhoe Society, we formed the Wivenhoe Preservation Trust, as a group, to raise money to try and protect Wivenhoe from further development on the scale of Wivenhoe Port. There was a big public inquiry in Wivenhoe, so we raised, I think it was £5,000 to pay for a barrister to represent Wivenhoe's interests at the public inquiry. We ended up with a complicated verdict, where I think all sides felt they'd gained something.

Peter Hill

The miners' strike

So, ultimately in the midst of all that, you had a miners' strike, which was frightening – actually led to the death of a policeman. Our stevedores had to run the gauntlet to get through into work each day.

It started off quite well. Some miners came up from Kent, and asked to see us, and said they wanted to picket our entrance – to protest against the coal imports, which we agreed to. They were nice chaps, and we agreed to let them park themselves outside the gate. We provided them with an oil drum, some timber, and some imported coal to keep them warm – which is slightly ironic!

Pat Alston

Scargill's lot

The coal imports weren't particularly new, but because the miners had gone on strike, the coal imports obviously started to build. They asked us to stop handling the coal, which we refused to do. But

The Miners' Strike, 1984-5 (Sue Murray).

it was very amicable. But then when the Yorkshire miners came down in bulk, Arthur Scargill's lot came down, and the whole picture changed.

Pat Alston

When I got up this morning I could hear something going on in the road so I walked through to the functions room to look. Out of the big bay window, and there were policemen as far as I could see, in both directions on both sides of the road, because the miners had come down to picket the Port. I looked out and thought, 'What on earth is going on?' And there were far more policemen than there were pickets!

Pat Smith

Divided loyalties

The miners were well supported by the local people, because they didn't like the Port anyway, so anything they could do to antagonise our business and make it difficult, was fine. They put the miners up, and looked after them, and brought them tea and stuff. But we had more than 500 pickets, miners, standing outside the gate. They had metal ball-bearings catapulted at drivers in lorries. Our employees were spat at and jeered at. There was a lot of police involvement. So that was awful, it was a difficult time. But we continued to handle the coal, because it was part of our business, and we had divided loyalties. Whatever sympathies you might have with miners, you have loyalty to your customers and the trade. So that's what we did.

Pat Alston

I kept a diary all the time and of course I blithely slagged the place off, saying, 'I wonder what the lads think when they get to Wivenhoe, with its fine pine and stripped wine, and Laura Ashley pots, and Laura Ashley bog-roll, and earthenware pots,' and it did rankle in a few corners.

Martin Newell

Yes, they were striking for what they believed was their right to do – which it was – and we had miners come in as customers and they were human beings as well as us, funnily enough! Unions have taken a back row over the years, but they've done many good jobs. It was not all strikes, it was fair wage for a fair day's work so that's fair enough.

Tony Allcock

During the miners' strike a lot of households took in groups of miners, we also did. We had great fun with them. They brought boxes of food which was given by their Union, none of which we liked – it was all things like corned beef and mushy peas. But they equally found us difficult because we had a tiny television and they couldn't believe that I was a schoolteacher living in such a small house with such a minimum equipment.

Janita Lefevre

The miners were friendly with us. But they were sorry for us because they said, 'I don't know what you're going to do in working, because our strike money is three times more than what you get as a week wages.'

Dave Weatherall

I was living in the Station Hotel during the Miners' Strike. And some of the policemen used to come in and have a drink with us and some of the miners did, and Fay laid the law down to the miners, she said, 'You're welcome to come in, as long as you don't picket or politics in the pub.' We were the meeting point, I think. Inside the pub was quite peaceable, but not outside! As soon as they reached the pub doors they had to wave the white flag, so we were quite proud of that really.

Colin Andrews

Split down the middle

Then I was president of the Sailing Club, and there was a lot of controversy. Several of us decided that we would throw our lot in with the 'Save Wivenhoe Campaign' or the 'Port Action Group.' And the Club split down the middle, around whether we should support the development, because it would bring more work to the town, or whether we should oppose it, which might mean the closure of the Port, and then the building of more houses there.

There were other issues too. It was the time of the miners' strike as well, and the coal being imported through the docks here. And we were very aware of all the environmental issues, with dusty cargoes being unloaded at the Port there. It was becoming a very industrial river, sailing felt very much marginalized, and more into a squeeze. We had to remove moorings so as to give room for the ships to berth at the Port, and the boats would get absolutely filthy with coal dust and fertilizer dust. So we felt we were being squeezed and restricted.

Alan Tyne

1989-94: The Barrier

While I was involved in the Wivenhoe Society, the biggest issue by far, was the barrier. We decided, as a society, that we ought to have a public meeting, in the British Legion Hall, and it was, literally, standing room only. There were as many people outside as in. The feeling of the village was against this blot on the landscape – as they saw it – which wasn't really there to benefit Wivenhoe, it was there to protect Colchester, so that they could build on the flood plain. There were pay-offs. Obviously the Sailing Club would have to move – they got a Sailing Club out of it. But that meeting was overwhelmingly against. Overwhelmingly against.

David Craze

And then about '89, there began to be talk of a barrier being built, and consultations started. Several of us, right from the day one, became convinced that they were going to do this – this was no consultation, they were going to do it, and that was all there was to it. And then it would be best if we tried to work out where the Club's interests lay, if they were going to do that. But there were some people who wanted to fight them and try and stop it from happening – and I could understand that. The whole idea is a complete abomination, and of no great practical use at all really, apart from people who want to build houses on land that's liable to flooding!

Alan Tyne

Talk with the devil

So whilst we might have sympathy with the view that the barrier should be resisted, on the other hand, we also had to try and talk with the devil and try and see what we could get out of this. So they eventually came up with a plan to provide us with the building that we now have – almost exactly as it is now. They gave us a 120-year lease, for £20,000, which is just a peppercorn rent. We had to raise about thirty-odd thousand pounds, and we had about £10,000/£15,000 in the bank, so we needed to raise the rest. So we got stuck into issuing loan notes, and running jumble sales and coffee mornings, and suddenly put the bar prices up, and we raised it with ease, and came out well ahead of ourselves.

Alan Tyne

Joggers, Websites and Mixing

I think Wivenhoe's become a bit more middle-class, you see people jogging along the path. You see people wearing Walkmans and sports clothes, puffing and panting along the cycle path and assiduously doing their exercise in the morning, and that's very kind of London parks and gardens, that, it's not really Wivenhoe. What are they doing? But it's still possible for me to go into Wivenhoe Woods and spend three-quarters of an hour there and maybe not see another soul.

Martin Newell

Wivenhoe website

I get a lot of satisfaction out of doing the website and the feedback. It's promoting people, it's promoting the artists, it's promoting the reputation of Wivenhoe. It's now grown to a point where it attracts over 500 visitors a week. You dip into it, in and out of it, which is why it's called the 'Wivenhoe Encyclopaedia.' I generally create between four and six pages a week trying to build a social history. One of the motivators for building a website was to build the social history of Wivenhoe because you look back and you can see all the events.

Peter Hill

A total mix

What I like about it is you have a total mix, and I can take friends or family down to, say, the Rose & Crown or the Black Buoy, and you do not know who you're talking to. It could be a professor, it could be the local fisherman. You just get the whole spectrum. And nobody goes on about who they are. I've so often been chatting away there, and they said, 'Did you know that person's a professor?' Or, 'Did you know that person goes out and fishes in the middle of the night.' That's been a nice aspect of the village and long may it carry on!

David Craze

ten

Still Sailing the Colne

Wivenhoe One-Designs racing, 1950s. (Glendower Jackson)

In the eighteenth century Wivenhoe's fishermen were already racing their smacks on the Colne for prizes given by the local gentry. For the races a key step was the introduction of the Wivenhoe One-Design dinghies in 1935. The Sailing Club was founded in 1925.

Sailing Club

The hut on the hard

We used to be on the Quay, there's the hut on the hard, that was the first place they had in 1936. That was brought down from Mr Pawsey's chicken farm in Spring Lane, and remounted down there, and varnished all out. And that was the sailing club until after the Second World War. Then we were upstairs in the British Legion, on the first floor. We were there until the barrier came.

Don Smith

In the 1950s we still had people like Dr Radcliffe on the committee, and Mr Worsp, business people in Wivenhoe. There was George Slaughter, who had the paper shop. Billy Cracknell, who was the baker. Dr Dean. Dr Radcliffe, of course.

Ray Hall

Quite a cross-section

It was a great Social Club, as well as everything else. Lots of cadets. When we were older and not cadet age, it was booming. We had super Christmas parties and New Year parties. It was quite full. Summer it was great. Cruise in company down the river, as far as East Mersea Stone, and that was great, we'd all meet down there.

There was quite a cross-section of people that belonged to the Sailing Club, that weren't sailors at all. Our old headmistress used to belong, Miss

Wivenhoe Sailing Club founders, 1925: Charles Scofield centre, Gibson Scofield last right, Charlie Sainty and Captain Billy Mason of Grosvenor Hotel also on right. (Nottage 1025)

Smith, with Miss Grasby, they lived together. I remember them making sandwiches down there, with cigarettes in their mouths, with great long ash on the end of it!

Jan Frostick

In the sixties, when the Club was still mostly dinghies, we used to have a 'Cruise in Company,' we used to go down to the Second Beach, over the St Osyth side, and we'd probably take forty, fifty people down, and we'd gather driftwood and have a damned great fire, and the ladies would fry up. We'd play cricket. Down there, the water's so clear, so clear. You see the bottom there at six, eight feet. And when we were down there, we used to go cockling and bring buckets home, and cook.

Don Smith

Instant friendship

The Sailing Club was a place where [when I came in 1975] I just fairly instantly found friendship. I'd always been interested in sailing. I was prepared for it to be aloof and distant, but I found it very welcoming and very open.

The boys would have been eight, nine, ten, eleven, they had a terrific time, because they joined the Cadet Section of the Sailing Club, and they began to do little trips and expeditions in their own rowing boat, they would go off, unaccompanied, down the river. The Cadets had languished a bit, and Jan and I took over, running it for a few years, and we ran a programme during the winter evenings.

Alan Tyne

A model for a club

I found the Club a comfortable place to be on a Friday evening, and the social events were great fun as well. We just took on organising roles, working parties to do maintenance and repairs, organising home-made events, like the talent night – people would stand up and read a poem, or sing a song or do a silly little act. And home-cooked evening meals, where everybody was invited.

As time went by, I began to see it as a kind of a model, for a voluntary organisation. I began to see it as a laboratory, in a way, to learn about how voluntary organisations worked! I remember Ralph Merry saying to me, very very early on, 'It's the work that's freely given that holds the place together.' People can always pay money for something, but there's no tie involved in that. When people have made it themselves, that means something to them, and they're going to look after it.

Alan Tyne

There was an opinion that the Wivenhoe Sailing Club had been *given* this new Club, by the River Authorities, which wasn't true. We had to find twenty thousand quid, the day we got the key, we had to give them a cheque for £20,000, and at that time, the membership was probably just over 200, so people bought shares, and bought life membership.

Don Smith

Still the same Club

Now it's still the same Club, but it just happens to be in a different building.

Alan Tyne

Then some of the chaps thought they'd like to put their boats out of the water, on the shore, for the winter, and so they formed a group, and they invested, and this group's been absorbed into the actual Club now, so we've got a tractor, and a big hoist for lifting the boats out and bringing them ashore, all the gear there, it's wonderful! The income from that is a great asset.

On the Quay at Regatta: Glendower Jackson is boy bottom left, Pat Ellis in white shirt, Mr Brown hairdresser standing, Dr Dean's Ford car. (Glendower Jackson)

Wivenhoe Sailing Club has taken a different shape, altogether now, because we've got about forty-odd cruisers in the Club. But we're still racing Wivenhoe One-Designs, which is wonderful, and some of these young wealthy people are spending thousands of pounds on having them being renovated. I like to see it, I think it's great.

Don Smith

Regatta

Apart from during the War, when I was a kid we always had a Regatta. There was one thing we always looked for and they finished up the Regatta with it – 'Pull devil, pull baker.' They had two teams from the fishing boats. One had bags of flour and one had bags of soot and they pelted each other! We used to love that when we were kids!

Freda Annis

The regattas always used to happen at the end of the sailing season when the yachtsmen were back for the season, and then they used to have the rowing races. When we were young, on Regatta days the Quay was full of people and Mr Macaulay used to bring down bales of straw for people to sit on and you used to have all sorts of activities. There was 'Pull devil, pull baker,' and 'Ducks and drakes,' they used to chase people across the marshes, and tug of war, and it was an event because there weren't many events in the village. A good day out it was.

Joyce Blackwood

The revived regatta

Well, for quite a few years, the traditional form of Regatta died out and it just became siling matches. But the Sailing Club have now decided that it's better they incorporate their regatta in with the Town Regatta, so that it's much more of

Wivenhoe Regatta, 1980s. (Nottage)

a community spirited thing now. The Wivenhoe Regatta Association was formed, and now they organise an event which includes shore-based and fun water events, like the shovel race, and there's a tug o' war which takes place in the mud, and other events which aren't necessarily nautical. But we still have the dinghy races and the cruiser and smack races.

Mike Downes

Sailing

Wivenhoe One-Designs

1936 was when they started, local people had them, business people, like the two doctors had one each, Mr Slaughter, and Mr Cracknell, Mr Worsp. It's a fifteen-foot dinghy, three-quarter deck. They're still sailing now. This was when Dr Radcliffe came here, and yacht designing was a hobby with him. It was a smaller version of the Brightlingsea One-Design of the 1920s, wasn't it? So they were ideal for the river, and the Estuary.

Prior to that, the Sailing Club had a mixed bag of boats, so it was a question of handicaps, which always caused arguments on decisions. The idea was quite common in Sailing Clubs all over the country, they have their One-Design, so they're all racing equally.

Pat Ellis, Joyce Blackwood and Don Smith

I used to race with Tony Frostick in number 12, *Sapphire*, and we could sort them out! I think Tony's name was on most trophies for a few years. A damned good sailor was Tony. Never any arguments. He only ever said about three words to me, as, 'Ready about? Lee-oh!' and the boat was there.

Ray Hall

I started my sailing in Wivenhoe One-Designs, because my father had a Wivenhoe One-Design built in the mid-thirties, No. 17 it is, so I sailed as soon as I was able to get aboard there! The Wivenhoe One-Design is very competitive. You sail for the Sykes Trophy and we sailed against Peter Sainty, who was a very good sailor. Crickey, yes!

Ken Green

Racing

To win dinghy races, you have to have a well tuned up boat with good sails, and you have to have a very good crew and work together as a team. You have to know the wind, and look out for wind shifts. The local conditions, you build up over the years. And keeping out the tide is very important. It's a tidal river, so obviously the mainstream of the tide is in the middle, and it's a lot more advantage to keep to the edges of the river if you can, without going aground. It's a balancing act, yes.

Stan Fenton

You should learn in a little dinghy, because then you become very aware of wind shifts, you realise that the wind isn't constantly running, it flutters and it either backs or veers a few degrees. And in the creeks and the rivers, over the years, you get to know where the little tidal eddies are. You work the wind shifts, the tidal eddies.

Tim Denham

But [the GPs, general purpose dinghies] they're not fast enough for the boys down at Brightlingsea! They want things where you're standing out like this, on the end of a wire.

A lot of the youngsters who learned here, felt their feet here, then moved on to Brightlingsea Club, where the racing was more exciting, because you race out to sea. But they learned how to do it here. Our local man, Malcolm Goodwin, was the one who really went to the top. He went down there, but still retained membership of the Club at Wivenhoe. But if you want traditional sailing with mud and the tide, then you stop at Wivenhoe.

Pat Ellis, Joyce Blackwood, and Don Smith

They never had no life-jackets, no buoyancy. Never had the rubber gear, no pansy gloves, no cleats. You hung on to the jib! Oh, that was all rough work!

Pat Ellis, Joyce Blackwood, and Don Smith

It was all cloth cap and plimsolls, and no waterproofs! I don't ever remember lifejackets. I think the first set of waterproofs I had was in 1959, these very heavy yellow plastics.

Ray Hall

Cruising and Day Sailing

We've got a cruising boat now, a Sadler 26. [When we were both retired] we went across the other side several times, for six weeks at a time, because we'd got the time to spare. And that was lovely, going all through the Dutch canals. We used to go round to Harwich and we've done the Deben, yes, and the Crouch, and the Blackwater. Woodbridge, Ipswich, and London, we sailed up to St Catherine's Dock, which was quite an experience, because there are all sorts of things in London that we'd had never seen, and we could do it with the boat as the base.

But now we're older, day sailing is quite enough. It's sometimes just four hours. One of the nice trips is sailing down with the tide, anchor off Mersea Stone, walk up to the Dog & Pheasant in Mersea, have something to eat, and a couple of pints, and come back and up with the tide back home. That's a lovely day out!

Pat Ellis and Joyce Blackwood

Boats with Histories

I was attracted by the type of sailing that was carried on in the estuaries, namely the sailing barges, coasting barges, small river barges, the big smacks, the small smacks, and the bawleys that do exist here, and don't exist at all, on the South Coast of England now. The Solent is just one sea of white plastic and speedboats. We're very lucky, in Essex, to have the rich and wide variety of different traditional sailing craft and there's a lot of historically very valuable craft on this part of the coast.

Crispin Yarker

balance, so he wasn't giving any consideration to how much room you had inside, he designed a boat that went, and then fitted everything out around it. She was built by Wistocks, round at Woodbridge, in 1939.

The one lady owner that owned her, '58 to'63, on the registration for the Admiralty, her profession was 'gentlewoman,' which I rather like! We've also had one author owned her, Simon Nolan, I've got one of his books on board.

You don't really own boats like this, you look after them for a period, and make sure they don't go downhill on your watch, and then they get handed on to someone else.

Andrew Cocks

Taloah

About 1980, we bought *Taloah*. She was a twenty-four foot, built in Wivenhoe, built at Cooks' shipyard, for the manager. In 1948, yes! The story was that they used up bits of timber that they put by during the War, when they were doing Admiralty contracts. The wood was good, the brass screws were lousy! She was designed by Maurice Griffiths, a famous East Coast yachtsman, who edited the *Yachting Monthly*, and lived locally. He wrote very evocative little essays about the pleasures of sailing round the salty muddy little creeks of the East Coast, rather than adventuring great distances abroad. He designed a number of very beautiful little boats.

She was a lovely old wooden boat, and I did a lot of boat repair work with her, and kept her at Guy Harding's yard on the front.

Alan Tyne

Metacentric yacht

I'm a member of the Wivenhoe and Rowhedge Yacht Owners' Association. My boat was designed by an amateur designer in 1939, Dr Thomas Harrison-Butler. He was an ophthalmist. He was obsessed with the 'metacentric' theory of yacht design. The idea was to build a boat with perfect

Saxonia

Three years ago I bought the *Saxonia*. She was built in 1930, for William Young & Son, to augment their fleet of existing bawleys based in Leigh-on-Sea. She was built by Aldous in Brightlingsea. She was the first bawley to be built with an engine. So she straddles that world of the pure wooden sailing boats and the modern motorised motor smacks. She's built of pitch pine, with an engine and a full sailing rig. And she was also the last of the stowboaters. She fished out of Leigh-on-Sea, for whitebait, until 1964. By then stowboating had become obsolete with the introduction of pair trawling, where you need powerful motor fishing boats, with the nets strung between them.

So she was sold to the Colchester Oyster Fishery Company, based in East Mersea, and worked for them as an oyster dredger, till about 1978/79, when she was converted back to her original sailing rig, and used as a private yacht. Her new owner, Jim Lawrence, chartered her all the time he'd owned her, which was about fifteen years. I've built up that business quite considerably, and last year, I did forty trips.

My initial interest is in maintaining the traditional skills of sailing a very heavy gaff-rigged boat, and keeping alive the skills of the rope work that's associated with these boats, and maintaining an awareness of how life used to be a hundred years ago.

Crispin Yarker

An ancient skill

I think it's an ancient craft, an ancient skill. I love little clinker boats, because, when I listen to the sound of the water chuckling under the bows, I think that our ancestors, the Vikings, would have heard that very same sound. And the thrill of going from A to B, just using the tides and the wind: it's a prehistoric skill that we can still practice.

Tim Denham

Yachtswoman

My father was a yachtsman. In the 1930s, when I was small, he was away most of the summer every year. Then in the winter, when he was at home, it was just touch and go whether he got a job or not, he went as a road worker. In the early days, he was on the King's yacht, *Britannia*, as one of the crew. The *Rosabelle* was the last one he was on, he stayed there until just before the war. When they went away for the summer season, the owner very often used to hand out little presents of cash for the boys and girls – sixpence for the boys, and the girls probably got threepence. I didn't really take up anything to do with the river myself, until I was over twenty. But I think it was always there, in the blood.

[Joyce started sailing with her friend Margaret in the 1950s.] Margaret bought a GP [general purpose dinghy], and we sailed that, we sailed all over the place. We took it to Wales, we took it to Cornwall, and we were known, in those days, because there weren't many women who sailed as a pair, we were known as 'The Girls,' wherever we went! And we always had a lot of help from all the men, putting the thing on a trailer and goodness knows what else. Then Margaret went off, and

then I started to sail with Pat [Ellis], and he'd got a GP.

Joyce Blackwood

Sailing and Ecology

Seals: fishermen versus sailing

The less said about them, the better! You don't get no fish. Yes, they take the herrings out your nets, and they also take the soles out your nets when you're trawling. Their numbers are increasing because of just being protected. There weren't so much talking, in the old days, about it, there was more action. There wasn't so many sailors, was there, about? There was only fishermen, or people doing commercial work. Now it's the other way around, isn't it? There's more people not earning a living, and finding time to report people, and feel sorry for things, which don't really involve them, does it?

Barry Green

The river is much cleaner

The river is much cleaner now. It's gotten better. You see cormorants up here now. And a seal comes up too. Years ago, there used to be a terrible discharge, all the time, from the gasworks at Colchester, used to come down the river. And you've no commercial craft coming up now. Because you used to get oil, too, on the water, with the commercial craft.

Don Smith

Hearing the birds and the rain

Another nice thing that we do now, it doesn't take long, we sail down to Pyefleet. There were seven or eight seals up there. The fishermen don't like them very much, but we all think they're very nice.

If you go on the water before high tide, when the mud is exposed, that's when you want to see all the birds. And now, there are hundreds of avocet and dippers and egrets. And herons. That's really lovely when you're down there. There's Rat Island as well, where the gulls all go, and we used to go on the island to pick up gulls' eggs. Of course, you're not allowed to do it in any more, but you'd get a bucket of gulls' eggs, and they made beautiful sponges!

At night, I don't sleep! That's why I can hear the birds! Oh, curlews, you hear them, and you hear the oyster catchers, which squeak as they fly, and they seem to be on the go all the time, the oyster catchers. And you definitely hear the rain! Oh God, yes, you hear the rain!

Pat Ellis and Joyce Blackwood

Just magical

I've always loved birds. And sailing, you can get so close. When you're at anchor, they'll come and perch on your boat. When you first see the terns – summer visitors – dropping into the river all round you, catching little shrimps and sand eels, it's just a lovely sight. And then you get magical flocks flying over. Even a bird as ordinary as the starling, they land and take off in large numbers on the marshes, and they fly in formation – when one turns, they all turn. Lots of the little shore birds – the ringed plovers, the sanderlings, the dunlin – they all have this skill of flying in fairly tight flocks and all turning at the same time, and one minute you see them brown, and the next minute you see them white, as they flit off in another direction, and somehow, it is just magical.

Some birds have disappeared a little. There used to be lots of little sparrows on the marshes, and they're not so common now. I think the lack of commercial shipping has had an influence on the river, and the bird that has reduced vastly in numbers is the swan, because while the shipping was here, they were unloading grain at Rowhedge and up at Colchester, so the spillage there was wonderful for the swans.

We've got the most romantic of all the geese on the Colne, the smallest goose in the world, and probably the wildest one, the brent goose, which breeds in Spitzbergen and North Russia, in Siberia, and it comes down here October time. Quite good to eat, they tell me, if you soak them in boiling water for twenty-four hours before you actually roast them! But I've not done it!

Cormorants were very very rare on the river, in fact so rare that when the fishermen went away as yacht crews, they came across them first in the Solent, standing on the end of the groynes, with their wings up drying, they nicknamed them 'Isle of Wight Parsons,' because of their black plumage and their white throat breathing pads. But now, of course, there are over 500 pairs at Abberton, and they're a complete nuisance!

Of course, on the river the one that I longed to see when I was little, was an avocet. The RSPB emblem is, of course, the avocet. I never saw one on the River Colne. Now we've got flocks of 450, and it's just wonderful to see them. They fly like butterflies, so elegant!

Tim Denham

The last wilderness

It's the last bit of real wilderness out there. When you're out there, midweek, there's nobody else there, and you really are living life to the full, pitting yourself against nature. And when the weather's beautiful, it's absolutely heaven on earth, and when the weather's awful, it's very exhilarating, very frightening, but very rewarding when you get safely back.

Tim Denham

John Bines and Ken Dadds working at James Cooke's. (John Bines)

eleven

James Dodds:
a New Fusion

James Dodds, Pioneer
in Frame, *1993: a
deep-sea smack built
on the Colne in 1864,*
Pioneer *was rescued
from the mud at West
Mersea and restored at
Great Totham between
1998-2001.*

I was born in 1957, in Brightlingsea, the eldest of four children. My father was an artist, he did black and white illustrations, from pen and ink drawings, for the *Radio Times*, and he used to get the train up to London once a week, to teach at St Martin's. He came from a farming family, and his first work was with the *Farmers Weekly*. My mother's family came from Brightlingsea.

When the railway closed we moved to Colchester, and I went to Stanway Secondary Modern School. I had a lot of difficulty reading and I compensated by drawing. The art room was my sanctuary at school. I left at fifteen.

Boatyard apprentice

At Brightlingsea, I was always envious of all the sailing going on. From fourteen I'd been working weekends on a sailing boat called the *Solvig*, a charter, sailed up and down all the rivers of the East Coast, and across to France and Holland, at that age quite an experience.

Then at fifteen I started an apprenticeship in Maldon, at Walter Cook and Sons, for four years. They wanted someone to follow on from Alf Last, boat-builder, who built barge boats, and smacks, he'd started work at something like thirteen, and at seventy-five retired! He rather resented me in the boatshed, he said, 'I'm not gonna tell you nothing. You've just got to watch me.' But I had about a year in with him. Then I went to Southampton for a year, to a shipbuilding training school, and I think that was when I realised I wasn't quite as stupid as I thought I was! All of a sudden, mathematics and lofting. I enjoyed lofting very much – where you draw out a boat, full-size, on the floor, and make moulds, and build your boat from those drawings. If you've got a mathematical formula to work out how many bits of wood you need to floor an area, suddenly maths makes sense!

Later on I used to go back and work at the yard in the summer holidays. I also worked with David Patience, in his own yard. Even when I left art school, the busiest time in the boatyard

was between Christmas and Easter, when nobody wants to sail, and as an artist, is the time when you don't sell any work, so it used to work out quite well. I'd get fit, and earn a bit of money. A lot of my boatyard lino cuts were of actual jobs that I'd worked on, so I could pretend to myself I was artist in residence, when I went back to work there! So I kept a connection going.

To Art School

While I was still in the Boatyard, I used to carry on doing evening classes in art. But really, after I'd finished my apprenticeship, and I'd been in a very male environment in the boatyard, there was a girl I fancied, who was going to art school, so I thought, 'Well, I'll have a go!' My father said, 'You're better off in the Boatyard. It's a very hard life.' But that just made me want to prove him wrong. I started at Colchester, a foundation year at Colchester and then got into Chelsea School of Art, and I did three years there, and then did another three years at the Royal College of Art, which I was very lucky to get in, there were only twelve places per year.

But I think, in a way, having had the boat-building and shipwrighting experience helped, was almost a better qualification than the O-Levels which I didn't have. It was only really in the final years at college, that I realised that the background that I'd got was very rich. And from that point onwards, I've been making pictures about the boatyards, and the construction of boats, and the subtlety of the shapes of boats, the regional variations, and how boat shapes have evolved to suit the kind of fishing and the kind of harbours and sea conditions in the region. All those shapes have evolved through experience and practice, rather than from an architect's table.

Coming to Wivenhoe

For me, as an artist, it's very important that I feel that I belong in an area. It gives a sense of security, but also a well of history to draw on. I first came

Wivenhoe about ten years ago, and built this house. It's a sail-loft type building, brick building, with accommodation upstairs and my studio downstairs. And then the family came along, and it all got a bit too crowded!

The lovely thing of coming to Wivenhoe, was when you were struggling with some painting or other, you could wander up the road and have a cup of coffee with someone, and they would tell you how they were struggling with what they were doing, and you'd go back feeling not so helpless. And if somebody came down from a gallery to Wivenhoe to buy a picture, and you can't sell them something, you take them round to somebody else's and they have a go at selling them something! There is a mutual support, professional and emotional.

Those two sides of me

When I was at the Royal College, I thought that I should become an intellectual, and I should be able to justify my pictures in historical or other terms. I felt that I had to embroider them with mythologies and stories, and justifications. Boats are so rich with associations, from the boat that carries you across the River Styx, and the idea of a church is based on a boat – the body of a church, the nave, isn't there a common origin of the word 'navy' and 'nave'? And there was a 'ship of fools,' that drifts aimlessly.

But it was having the opportunity of a big show at the Minories that really helped focus me on what was unique to my view of the world. I thought, 'I've got this big space to fill. What can I do?' I painted a big boat over a painting which I'd been struggling over for six or seven years, it was a completely unresolved picture, and I resolved it by painting this big blue boat over the top of it. And it was so enjoyable, it felt easy, because I understood the construction of the boat, it was as if I was building the boat while I was painting it. So I thought, 'I'll do some more of those!' not thinking that they would sell, just that it would make a good theme for the show, and it fitted with my story, and to my

surprise, they sold! And I can't paint them quick enough at the moment!

Most of them are done from a very specific viewpoint, I like to think it's the view that the boat-builder would have when they were building the boats. The boats would be up on the stocks, and the sheer line would be at eye level. I like the physicality and the solidness of the boats, and the curvaceousness, and I like to show how they're constructed. Some of the first paintings of the boats were almost life-size, and that certainly adds to their power, being that big, but their strangeness as well, when they're almost of hovering on the wall.

For a long time, I felt a great division between the boat-builder part of me, and the artist part of me, and I kept them very much apart, and thought that they were two separate worlds. And one of the nice things, again, about painting the boats, is that those two sides of me have come together. At the age of forty-eight, I'm, at last, happy with who I am. I'm a boat-builder and an artist. I'm very lucky and pleased with that.

Book Contributors

Tony Allcock, born Colchester 1938, came to Wivenhoe in 1959 and runs the Allcock & Stevens electrical and television shop.

Pat Alston, born Colchester 1949; secretary at Wivenhoe Port.

Colin Andrews, born Reepham, Norfolk 1940, came to Wivenhoe in 1967. Worked as a railwayman before running the Station Hotel in Wivenhoe. Today a housepainter and builder.

Freda Annis, born 1917, into an old Wivenhoe family. Shop assistant in Wivenhoe.

John Ashworth, born Luton 1938, came to Wivenhoe 1973 as Professor of Biology at Essex University, Chief Scientist to the Cabinet Office and Chairman of the British Library.

Roger Bacon, born Colchester 1930, moved to Wivenhoe in 1936. Teacher and cricketer. [Also recorded with Cricket Club interview.]

Austin Baines, born Kenilworth 1936. Librarian at Essex University, Secretary of Wivenhoe Society and Town Councillor.

Eunice Baker, born Colchester 1923, came to Wivenhoe in 1935. Farm worker, steward at Arts Club.

Richard Barnard, born 1953, came to Essex University and then Wivenhoe in 1974. Teacher, active in Sailing Club.

Hilda Barrell, born Fingringhoe *c.* 1895, arrived Wivenhoe aged 18 months. Member of a farming and maritime family, spending childhood on Wivenhoe Quay. [Interviewed by Diana Gittins *c.* 1975]

John Barton, born Colchester 1946, came to Wivenhoe 1951. Coach driver for Cedrics from 1977.

Penny Bell, born Kirby Cross, 1940. Co-founder of Wivenhoe Bookshop in 1976.

Leila Berg, born Salford 1917, came to Wivenhoe 1985. Writer and political activist.

Annie Bielecka, born Criccieth, N. Wales 1945, daughter of a seaman. Came to Wivenhoe 1975. Social worker, now artist.

Phil Bingham, born Norfolk 1946, came to Wivenhoe 1972. Worked in computing, became a Methodist lay preacher.

John Bines, born Colchester 1934. Worked at Cook's shipyard 1950-1986.

Joyce Blackwood, born Wivenhoe 1928. Daughter of a yachtsman, became a teacher and a pioneer woman sailor.

John Bowes, born at Ballast Quay Farm, Wivenhoe, 1936. Took over farm from father in the 1960s.

Shirley Bowes, born Colchester 1938. Farmer's wife at Ballast Quay Farm.

Rodney Bowes, born Colchester 1960, son of John Bowes and grandson of Ernie Vince. Fisherman.

Brian Buckle, born Suffolk 1933, came to Wivenhoe 1935; father head horseman on Wivenhoe Park Estate. Worked on the estate from 1947, rising to be foreman.

David Burrows, born 1940 and **Jean Burrows** came to Wivenhoe 1986 and ran the Post Office at the Cross for twenty years.

Nicholas Butler, born and came to Wivenhoe in 1936, son of actress Joan Hickson, journalist, and Wivenhoe historian.

Lyn Button, born Glasgow 1947, came to Wivenhoe 1974. Teacher at Broomgrove School since 1979.

Richard Chopping, born Colchester 1917, moved to Wivenhoe 1945 with Dennis Wirth-Miller. Pioneer of artists' community in Wivenhoe.

Andrew Cocks, born West Mersea 1952, Colchester publisher. Yachtsman, active member of Wivenhoe and Rowhedge Yacht Owners' Association.

Patricia Coventry, born Essex 1937, came to Wivenhoe in 1972. Active Congregationalist

David Craze, born London 1947, teacher. Former Mayor of Wivenhoe, keen collector especially of Wivenhoe postcards.

Pam Dan, born 1939, came to Wivenhoe 1954. Artist; wife of potter John Dan; involved with Arts Club.

Tim Denham, born Wivenhoe 1935. Teacher, sailor and ornithologist.

James Dodds, born Brightlingsea, 1957, moved to Wivenhoe 1995. Son of an artist, trained as shipwright before going to art school.

Barbara Donohue, born Wivenhoe 1924. Active Congregationalist.

Mike Downes, born 1940, has lived Wivenhoe since 1980. Photographer and printer. Since 1992 Warden of Nottage.

Helen Douzier, born 1947, ran a hairdressing business in Wivenhoe High Street. Treasurer of Wivenhoe Congregational Church.

Leonard Drinkell, born Wivenhoe 1927. Colchester auctioneer, keen cricketer, Mason.

Peter and Diane Duffield, Peter, born Messing 1936, Diane, born Tollesbury 1941. Came to Wivenhoe 1963; involved with Allotments Association and Wivenhoe Show.

Clare Durance, born 1947, came to Wivenhoe 1972. Co-founder of Gilbert and Sullivan Society in 1980. Teacher.

Jim Dutton, born at Sunnymede Farm, Wivenhoe 1934. Took over from father who farmed there from 1931.

Linda Edwardson, born in Southend 1949, came to Wivenhoe in 1988. Runs Londis shop in Vine Parade, Active role in annual pantomime.

Bill Ellis, born Ilford 1925. City banker, retired to Wivenhoe 1975. Secretary and treasurer of Nottage Institute 1977-95.

Patrick Ellis, born Wivenhoe 1924, father ran a chandler's shop. Pat became ship's engineer.

Phil Faucheux, born Kent 1923, son of a master canner, moved to Wivenhoe 1924. Railway fitter. Secretary of Allotments Association and Wivenhoe Show 1959-76, secretary and groundsman of Cricket Club.

Stan Fenton, born Wivenhoe 1957. Electrician. Active in Wivenhoe Sailing Club.

Louis Footring, came to Wivenhoe 1961. Radio officer on cross-channel ferries. Involved with Arts Club.

Tony Forsgate, born Wivenhoe 1929. Teacher. Cricket Club Secretary 1952 – 69.

Sheila Foster, born Kent 1950, came to Wivenhoe 1974. Theatre background, involved with various Wivenhoe drama groups including Players and Youth Theatre.

Jan Frostick, born Chester 1940, came to Wivenhoe. Hairdressing business in Wivenhoe in 1960s.

Tony Frostick, born Wivenhoe 1938. Ship's draughtsman at Rowhedge. Later worked for Marconi and BT; active member of Wivenhoe Sailing Club.

Joan Gifford, born in South Africa 1927, came to Wivenhoe 1991, Folk Club activist, teaches guitar.

Mary Girling, born Brightlingsea 1943, farmer's daughter and deerhound breeder. Was departmental secretary in sociology at Essex University.

Marjorie Goldstraw, born Wivenhoe 1921. Family ran dairy and manned tollgate. Clothing factory worker.

Annabel Gooch, born Oxford 1939, married Charles Gooch 1961. Continues to live at Tye Farm on Wivenhoe Park Estate.

Betty Govan, born Wivenhoe 1928. Grew up at Ballast Quay Farm; later shop worker and British Legion activist.

Alan Green, born Wivenhoe 1930. Railway mechanic. Involved with Scouting movement for forty years.

Barry Green, born Wivenhoe 1942. Worked for Cook's Shipyard as welder. Part-time fishing skipper.

Brian Green, born Wivenhoe 1932, started fishing at fifteen. From 1965 fish and chip shopkeeper, ran business thirty-six years.

Carol Green, born London 1936, came to Wivenhoe 1978. Worked in family shop. Involved in crabbing competition and charity fund raising.

Ken Green, born Wivenhoe 1934. Fisherman and fish salesman.

Pat Green, born Wivenhoe 1938. Kept greengrocers shop in High Street.

Peter Green, born Wivenhoe 1932. Fisherman and fish retailer.

Ray Hall, born Wivenhoe 1937. Shipyard apprentice, heating engineer. Involved in air-sea rescue and Sailing Club.

Canon Stephen Hardie, born Bedford 1941. Rector of Wivenhoe 1976-92. Involved in Gilbert and Sullivan productions and sailing.

Jean Harding, born Manchester 1923. Co-founder of Wivenhoe Bookshop in 1976.

Hilary Harvey, born Rowhedge 1950, but family worked in Wivenhoe shipyard. Has memories of sport in Wivenhoe.

Brian Heasman, born 1935, came from Suffolk to Wivenhoe 1972, working for British Telecom. Active Mason.

Bill and Enid Heslop, born 1936 and 1938, both from County Durham, moved to Wivenhoe 1963. Bill is an artist and retired former art teacher.

Peter Hill, born Southend-on-Sea 1950. Works in city business. Came to Wivenhoe in 1972. Active participant in Town Council, Scout and Guide Association, Engine Shed Project and many Wivenhoe organisations.

Celia Hirst, born Redditch 1953. Came to Wivenhoe, 1975. Blues and jazz singer, founder-organiser of May Fair.

Frank Hodgson, born West Hartlepool 1923. Manager at Cook's Shipyard. Active with Wivenhoe Bowls Club.

Glendower Jackson, born Swindon 1931, came same year to Wivenhoe. Worked as electrician and for Foreign Office. Collector of Wivenhoe postcards.

Sue Kerr, born Colchester 1934, soon moved to Wivenhoe. Physiotherapist. Father ran butchers' shops in Colchester and Wivenhoe.

Ivy Knappett, born Wivenhoe 1908, daughter of shipyard riveter. First job picking out sprats on Quay. Farm worker.

Jimmy Lawrence, born Colchester 1933. Worked on barges. Sailmaker, teacher at Nottage.

Janita Lefevre, born 1950, moved Wivenhoe 1974. Humanities teacher. Works for education in Ethiopia.

Pat Moss, born Stratford 1932, evacuated to Wivenhoe in war. Active Congregationalist.

Martin Newell, born Hertfordshire 1953, moved to Wivenhoe in 1975. Poet and performer. Author of *The Wild Man of Wivenhoe*.

Halcyon Palmer, born Shropshire 1934, daughter of Dr William Dean who practised in Wivenhoe from 1935. Her mother Margery Dean was first socialist local councillor and antique dealer.

Dr Ted Palmer, born Chichester 1931, came to Wivenhoe in 1963 as GP, married Halcyon. Founder member of Wivenhoe Society; enjoys collecting antiques.

Ken Plummer, born London 1946, came to Wivenhoe 1975, Sociology Professor at Essex University.

Ellen Primm, born Wivenhoe 1920, daughter of shipyard worker. Worked as tailoress and in wartime as shipyard carpenter.

Ann Quarrie, born Grimsby 1950s, set up an estate agency in Wivenhoe in 1988. Town Councillor.

Muriel Ryder, born West Hartlepool 1922. Employed at Wivenhoe Park House in 1930s as servant. [Colchester Recalled interview]

Charles and June Sansom, born in 1919 and 1923, came to Wivenhoe in 1948. Charles a shipyard plater, June worked in electrical assembly and later at Essex University.

Peter Sainty, born Wivenhoe 1930, from local maritime family. Architect.

Charles Scofield, born Wivenhoe 1930. Family in painting and decorating trade. Worked in housing. Active with Masons, Bowls and Cricket Clubs.

Annie Skilton, born Wivenhoe 1918. One of thirteen children; worked for North Sea Canners from age 14; later with husband for Skilton and West's transformer business.

Don Smith, born Wivenhoe 1923. Shipyard engineer 1940s-50s; water engineer 1960s. Active in Wivenhoe Sailing Club.

Pat Smith, born Colchester 1933, came to Wivenhoe in 1979. Ran Greyhound pub 1980s, active on Wivenhoe Society Committee.

Dennis Sparling, born Wivenhoe 1931. Childhood at Station Hotel. Later Colchester engineer.

William Sparrow, born Wivenhoe 1962, grandson of landlord of Rose and Crown, runs family building business.

Max Tannahill, born in County Down, Ireland 1959. Artist, moved to Wivenhoe in 1989.

Guy Taplin, born London 1939, came to Wivenhoe in 1976. Artist.

Charles Tayler, born Alresford 1922. Moved to Wivenhoe in 1929. Baker and lorry driver.

Hilda Taylor, born in Lancashire 1926, came to Wivenhoe in 1970. Headteacher Broomgrove School. Quaker, active in peace movement and overseas charities.

Rev David Thomas, born Warrington 1950. Rector of Wivenhoe since 1992.

Janet Turner, born in Persian Gulf 1945, came to Wivenhoe 1975. Co-founder of Gilbert and Sullivan Society; keen sailor.

Alan Tyne, born East London 1945, came to Wivenhoe 1973. Social worker, active in Sailing Club, also runs charities for disabled.

Ernie Vince, born Elmstead Market 1911, moved to Wivenhoe 1917. Fisherman, barge and yacht skipper.

Graham Wadley, born Hertfordshire 1946, came to Wivenhoe 1954. Chartered Mechanical Engineer. Musical director of St Mary's church.

Dave Weatherall, born Pembrokeshire 1937, came to Wivenhoe in 1957. Worked as baker then electrician.

Sylvia Weatherall, born East London 1936. Worked at North Sea Canners and later as library assistant at Essex University.

Bill Webb, born Suffolk 1922, shipyard draughtsman in Rowhedge and Wivenhoe in 1940s.

Gilbert Whaley, born Lancashire 1920. His father, plumber, moved to Wivenhoe 1930 to find work. Carpenter.

Olive Whaley, born Wivenhoe 1931. Writes historical novels under pen-name Elizabeth Jeffrey.

Tom Wiseman, born Essex 1916. Primary teacher in Wivenhoe 1938 and 1946.

Walter Wix, born Wivenhoe 1921. Manager/foreman at Loveless sandpits.

Sir Peregrine Worsthorne, born 1923. Journalist. Involved with Wivenhoe Arts Club.

Crispin Yarker, born London 1954. Professional musician, owner and skipper of *Saxonia* fishing smack.

We wish to thank the following for also giving interviews for the project:

Amy Barrell, Jack Barrell, Marjorie Barton, Emma Baxter, Jean Blackwell, Joanna and Richard Bornat, Mark Britten, Agnes Buckle, Joan Busfield, Peggy Carrington, Dr Peter Chapman, Dot Chaney, Jacqueline Claiborne, Annabel Cole, Sid Cox, Ann Dale, Jack Diggens, John Dowden, Peggy Elliott, Peter Frank, Pam Glover, John Greenman, John Harris, Harry Hatch, Leslie Kemble, Maurice Kimmit, Penny Kraft, David Lee, Leonore and David Lockwood, Philip Long, Canon Bill Loveless, Alistair McAuley, Val Mainwood, Jack Mallett, Ralph Moss, Janet Noyes, Mark Patterson, Rod Pawsey, Pat and Geoff Pearce, Gabriel Pearson, Elsie Pleasance, Gilly Poole, Sandra Putt, Sheila Quinney, Paul Ridley-Thomas, Peter Sainty, Minnie Scott, Brian Sinclair, William Sparrow, John and Winnie Street, Jan Tyne, Edna Wadley, Paul Walker, Tom Webb, Roland Wheeler, Jennifer White.

We are also grateful to the following recorded in groups or in brief recordings at special Wivenhoe events:

Bowls Club group: Frank Hodgson, Charles Scofield.

Cricket Club group: Roger Bacon, Mark Britten, Len Drinkell, Paul Evans, Tony Forsgate, Nigel Philp, Terri Philp.

Colne Lodge Freemasons group: Len Drinkell, Brian Heasman, Alex Paterson, Charles Scofield.

Valley Road group: Maggie Bernstein, Joyce Grey, Gisela Langsdorff-Barnard, Christine Lee, Pat Marsden, Janet Turner.

Art on the Railings and June Market brief interviews: Meriel Empson, Steve Ford, Connie Haken, Bonnie Hill, Julie Howe, Pauline McColl, Graeme Martin, June Mayhew, Joe Rampling, Kathy Warr, Ginny Waters, Anthony Wells, John Williams.

Open Gardens brief interviews: Michael Anderson, Angela Charnock, Clare Durance, Connie Riley, Sandra Smith, Richard Sykes, Jan Thurlow, Wayne Ward, Alison Webster, Ray Woodcock.

Crabbing Competition brief interviews: Chris Barnham, Camille Corti-Georgiou, Sarah Elmstead, Barry Green, Nina O'Shea, Louise Richards, Frances Richards.

Wivenhoe Town Regatta brief interviews: Libby Armstrong, Nick Baker, Fabian Bush, Andrew Cocks, Jane Cole, Mike Downes, Shelley Faucheux, Stan Fenton, Howard Field, Jean Gale, Bonnie Hill, Jane Nicholas.